D0294755

THE
LANCASHIRE
LIBRARY

FOR REFERENCE

ONLY

A HISTORY OF POLICING
IN
MANCHESTER

A HISTORY OF
POLICING
IN
MANCHESTER

By
ERIC J. HEWITT

1979
E. J. Morten (Publishers)
Didsbury, Manchester, England

A HISTORY OF POLICING IN MANCHESTER
First Published November 1979 by
E. J. Morten (Publishers). A division of
E. J. Morten (Booksellers) Ltd, 6 Warburton Street,
Disbury, Manchester 20, England

© E. J. Hewitt. 1979

© Illustrations; copyright retained by the original owners. 1979

I.S.B.N. 0-85972-040-3

Printed in Great Britain by
The Scolar Press Ilkley Yorkshire

CONTENTS

To June, with love.

A HISTORY OF POLICING IN MANCHESTER

LIST OF ILLUSTRATIONS

Photographs assembled with the assistance of members of the Display and Exhibition unit, and reproduced by kind permission of the Chief Constable of Greater Manchester Police.

INTRODUCTION

The great problem of English police-work has long been the difficulty of reconciling effective police action with individual freedom of action. In Manchester, prior to the epoch of Industrial Revolution, an uneasy compromise existed whereby the constables were employed on a voluntary basis and with their fellows' cooperation, to manage the township, with occasional resort to the military in emergency.

The demographic explosion and the onset of large-scale urbanisation deprived the township of this ancient advantage and criminal disorder pressed hard on Manchester's outmoded and ill-equipped system of local government. Expanding commerce created its own range of possible thefts; frequently dire want was a major factor; the drink and prostitution traffic were fostered by expanding town life; criminal tendencies seem to have been stimulated by the often degrading social milieu and there was the new danger of proletarian mass-action, with its consequent threat to property. By the late 1830's the situation was apparently out of hand. Although punishment was brutal and severe, the balance in the centuries-old struggle between law and crime favoured the criminal. It was in these discouraging conditions that Manchester prepared itself for police reform.

The proponents of the police idea made little headway against the tide of public opinion. One Parliamentary Committee after another rejected it. "Such a system", reported one Committee in 1818, "would of necessity be odious and repulsive. It would be a plan which would make every servant of every house a spy on the actions of his master and all classes of society spies on each other".

Home Secretary Peel had long been attracted by the ideas of Police Reformers and he would easily sympathise with the new anxieties of factory owners and shopkeepers. He was well aware of the only conditions on which the English could be persuaded to accept police. To overcome the hostility of centuries the system would have to be conceived from the start as a service.

The first Police Commissioners were instructed to recruit men who would be loyal and honest, but who need not be too intelligent. When the first recruits appeared on the streets of London in September 1829, they were seen to be carrying only wooden batons and they wore top hats and belted blue coats. Anything less military would be difficult to imagine, and their first instructions directed them to be civil and obliging to all persons, whatever their rank or class. The recruit was informed that the most indispensable qualification was that he must at all times have a perfect command of his temper, and that it was fundamental to the work to secure and to retain the goodwill of the public. The police were first and foremost a preventative force. They were, as today, neither an arm of the executive nor an instrument of repression.

Manchester followed the Metropolitan example a decade later when the township was incorporated under the terms of the Municipal Corporations Act. The new Borough had a very stormy baptism, during which the Crown had to intervene and install a Chief Commissioner of Police. The new Borough finally settled its differences and established its own Police Force under the appointed leadership of Captain Edward Willis, its first Chief Constable.

There was little that was "new" about Manchester's new police force. A certain amount of continuity with the past prevailed for several years with many of the old watchmen and manorial officers holding office in the Borough Constabulary Force. Nonetheless, the reform of the police appears to have righted the balance between law and crime. Thereafter, the tide of crime was stemmed, if not turned back.

Possibly the greatest achievement of the early Chief Constables was the relaxation of tension in respect of public disorder. Their success in this area of their responsibilities was even more decisive than their activities in the prevention of crime, which themselves were creditable.

From the time the force came into existence, the orgies of destruction which had characterised the large-scale riots in the 18th and early 19th centuries and which often terminated in bloody conflicts with the military became a thing of the past. The first great test came in 1848 when the last of a series of Chartist outbursts were dispersed without having to resort to military force. These new-fangled tactics of the police made for duller history, but less frequent bloodshed.

There is no single explanation of the force's development in the second half of the century. If any consistency can be observed it must be the prime consideration given to the basic principles of local government. Finance constantly entered the reckoning, as council and ratepayers fought shy of increased expenditure. On the other hand, there was the ratepayer's natural wish to ensure security for the community to which he belonged, as well as the growing pride in municipal institutions. The local authority then, as today, was primarily concerned with that precarious juggling of prestige, efficiency and economy which has been the hallmark of local rule.

The 19th century closed with one of the city's most senior police officers in the centre of a grave public scandal which threatened the balance of power between the Watch Committee and its Chief Constable.

The underlying conflict came to be resolved with the appointment of Robert Peacock as Chief Constable. Under his dynamic and skilful leadership the force was reorganised. He speedily put an end to deplorable practices which he found to exist. On one occasion several Magistrates turned up at Court, as if by accident, and sat on the Bench during a case in which certain publicans with whom they were on friendly terms were being prosecuted. After considerable public debate, Peacock eventually secured the resignation of the Magistrates concerned. During this era the mid-Victorian policeman for all his worth, receded as far back into history as the watchman had long ago receded from him.

The inter-war years were notable for the chronic economic depression which threw millions out of work and crippled thousands of businesses. During 1926, the year of the General Strike, Manchester's police force was stretched to its limit as public frustration manifested itself in a series of marches and demonstrations. The police proved so successful in handling this volatile and extremely sensitive situation that a number of local Trades Unions and Worker's Organisations placed on record their appreciation of the tolerant and good humoured approach shown by their fellow workers in uniform.

In more modern times the most obvious and general change has been the progressive disappearance of the constable on the beat and the appearance in his place of the constable in the patrol car. This was considered necessary because of the growing shortage of recruits for the force, and also by the growth in number and gravity of crimes which depend for their execution upon the use by criminals of lorries and fast cars (usually stolen). Despite the obvious benefits to be derived from a greater mobility, the "panda car" had the predictable consequence that it cut the policeman off from the community and spread a feeling of insecurity among the public at large.

Between the years 1968-74 Manchester's City Police became embroiled in two amalgamations each designed to restructure local government in line with the changes which had taken place in post-war society. The first involved close neighbours Salford who had successfully avoided similar schemes in the past. The second amalgamation involved Manchester and Salford as member constituents of the newly created Greater Manchester County. The 6000 strong Greater Manchester Police, covering an area which a few years before had been policed by ten separate forces, became the largest provincial police in England.

It has been remarked that the early nineteenth century reformers were brought to a realization that the reform of the police was essential if the wave of criminality was to be halted. Once again we are living in an age when much crime remains undetected or unsolved, when many rogues escape conviction and when many of our main thoroughfares are travelled at night-time by gangs of young robbers not averse to the deployment of crude violence on their helpless victims.

Whether the present situation calls forth a radical or a reformist solution is a question for future historians to contemplate. What remains clear in today's changing and uncertain society, is that the role of the police is no less crucial than at any other time in its history.

The whole complex story of police in Manchester has been pieced together from a plethora of documentation, newspaper reports and historical writings. It is long overdue. Although the central theme has been the police and its growth from the old watch system, I have tried to show how the police developed side by side with the township, occasionally reflecting the social, economic and political trends during each epoch.

My sincere thanks go to my sister-in-law Mrs. Lynne Thompson for her dedicated assistance in typing the script.

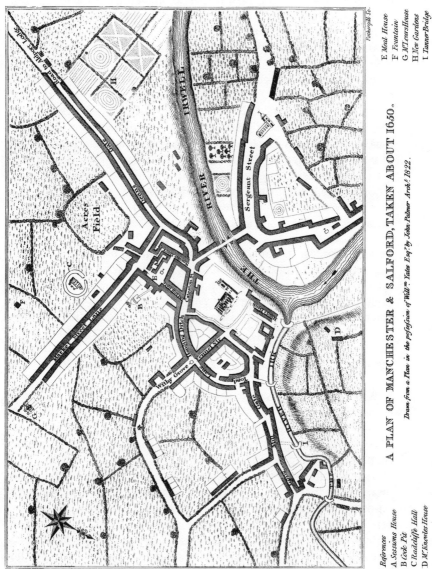

A PLAN OF MANCHESTER & SALFORD, TAKEN ABOUT 1650.

Drawn from a Plan in the possession of W.m Yates Esq.r by John Palmer Arch.t 1822.

References
A Sessions House
B Cook Pit
C Radcliffe Hall
D M.r Knowles House
E Meal House
F Fountain
G M.r Cross House
H New Gardens
I Tanner Bridge

Chapter One

EARLY BEGINNINGS – COURT LEET AND POLICE COMMISSIONERS

To obtain a vivid picture of everyday life in the township of Manchester, we may turn to the records of the Court Leet, of which an almost unbroken series has been preserved from 1552 down to the municipal purchase of the manorial rights in 1846.

The Manchester Court Leet was a hybrid court, descended on the one side from the half yearly full sessions of the Medieval Court Baron, and descended on the other from the old Portmoot which met four times a year to transact business relating to the town and its burgesses. It became, quite simply, a court for the town of Manchester and its hamlets.

Thanks to a printed plan we know exactly how the township looked as early as 1650. The Collegiate Church forms the focal point of the town, and from this centre three main streets stretched into the fields. One, 'Long Millgate' went north along the bank of the Irk past the corn mills; the second, 'Deansgate' went south about as far as today's Peter Street junction; the third, 'Market Stead Lane' (now Market Street), went eastwards, with shops and houses on either side backed by fields and at the end, after about a quarter of a mile, stood Mr. Lever's house, roughly where Barratt's shoe shop is today.

There were two market places and between them stood the Session House where the Court Leet met.

Although the Court was manorial in form, its jurors were all burgesses of the town; moreover, the numerous officers annually appointed by the Court were also all Burgesses. Of these officers most were unpaid, but some of the inferior officers performing more menial services evidently received fees or perquisites.

Of the unpaid officers the first to be elected was always the Boroughreeve, who was the chief officer of the town, and most nearly corresponded to the Mayor of a borough. By the 16th

13

century his office had become honorary rather than active. Some of his duties were now being performed by the catchpole or Bailiff of the Court Leet, a paid officer who "risked his skin" collecting fines and carrying out the distraints according to orders made by the jury "unto good and lawful purposes for the reforming, and avoiding of divers trespasses and offences." The catchpole was theoretically the deputy of the boroughreeve, and was regularly appointed at each Michaelmas Court Leet, immediately after the boroughreeve, but this annual election was from the beginning not much more than a formality. In actual practice, he kept his office indefinitely, so long as he was able to do his duty to the satisfaction of the boroughreeve.

The most important executive functions of local administration were exercised by the two constables, who (like the boroughreeve) were annually − elected, and unpaid officers of the Court Leet. The constables of Manchester were responsible, in general, for the maintenance of peace and order in the town, and for the execution of orders made by the Court Leet or by the County Magistrates. Like the constable of other manors or townships, they were to arrest all felons and persons "making Riots, Debates, or Frays, or breaking the Peace," and to enforce the statutes concerning "Watch, Hue and Cry, Sturdy Beggars, Vagabonds, Rogues, and other Idle Persons," including persons who played unlawful games. They were sworn to execute all processes and warrants sent to them from the Justices of the Peace of the County, and to make "good and faithful presentment of all Blood-sheds, Out-crys, Affrays, and Rescues."[1] It is also to be remembered that, down to the later 16th century, it was the constables and not the churchwardens who were responsible for supervising the control of beggars, the lodging of the impotent poor, and the apprenticing of poor children.

In the performance of their onerous and responsible duties the Manchester constables had at first no special paid assistant, though they received some incidental help from the catchpole. There was, of course, a general understanding that every townsman should be ready to aid the constables at any time, by day or by night, and this obligation was from time to time emphasised in special orders of the Court Leet, but this casual sort of assistance can hardly have been adequate to the needs of a growing town, which was increasingly the resort of "Light and Evil-disposed Persons" and of "Strangers that make Brawls."[2]

For the protection of the town by night the constables had the right to summon any townsman to serve as a night watchman in his turn, or to send a "sufficient" substitute. In practice this came to mean the employment of privately paid watchmen, and this in turn led eventually to the direct employment of regular watchmen paid by the constables out of local rates.

After 1614 the constables had the assistance of a paid "Beadle or Marshall" who received such wages or stipend as was thought proper by the steward, boroughbreeve, and constables, and as a perquisite to his wages he was to receive 4d. for every rogue he whipped. In addition, he was provided with his uniform equipment; a good cloth coat faced with yellow kersey. together with a hat or cap, a whip, and an official staff with a knob on it. [3] The staff was painted or gilded, and the coat seems to have been adorned with four dozen buttons; the hat and coat were apparently renewed each year. The beadle's stipend may appear ludicrously small in comparison with the resplendence of his uniform, but it is to be remembered that whippings were frequent in those days; in a brisk year the beadle might average more than one whipping in each week. In the single year 1618-19 the constables of Manchester paid for seventy-four shippings.[4]

In the appointment of a paid beadle may be found one of the beginnings of the modern police force of Manchester; yet the office, in its early days, seems to have been curiously intermittent and casual. The beadle may originally have been an unpaid officer of the Court Leet, receiving merely occasional fees for special services; as early as 1573 the jury of the court appointed Adam Johnson as "Beadle for the Rogues," and he was still holding the office three years later. Thereafter the appointment lapsed, and the engagement of a paid beadle in 1614 was a fresh start, under new conditions of appointment and service. In the first instance appointment was presumably by the steward, boroughreeve and constables, who were jointly responsible for fixing the rate of pay; but later appointments were left in the hands of the constables, while the rate of pay was fixed by the Court Leet.

As their general assistant the constables employed a deputy constable, who began on somewhat the same footing as the beadle, but later became the professional forerunner of the modern Chief Constable as the effective head of the Manchester police force. The constables were employing a deputy constable at least as early as 1616, though they did not as yet pay him a fixed stipend; he received merely occasional fees and his expenses for such services as raising the "Hue and Cry" against horsestealers and housebreakers.[5] By 1624, however, he was receiving a yearly allowance of £1. 0. 0. in addition to his occasional fees and expenses, which soon amounted to several times as much as the regular allowance.[6] The importance of his office evidently increased very rapidly. In 1638 the jury of the Court Leet being "informed that William Shelmerdine, Deputy Constable, is a man painful in his place, and yet not rewarded accorded to his pains," ordered that he should have a quarterly allowance of 10s. 0d. "out of the leys or assessments of the town, for his pains taking in the town's business." Henceforward the deputy constable may be regarded as an officer of the Court Leet, and his importance greatly strengthened.

During the succeeding period of civil warfare and social unrest the special fees of the deputy constable naturally became a heavier burden on the dwindling resources of the town. It was partly because of this economic reason that the Court Leet decided to give Shelmerdine a higher inclusive salary, instead of paying his "per Particular." In 1648, when the tide of war had receded from the town, the Court Leet ordered that in future "the said Deputy Constable that shall be made choice of by and for the assistance of these constables, shall have for all the service and attendance due and appertaining to the said office of Deputy Constable the sum of ten pounds per annum, and that to be paid by fifty shillings per quarter."[7] The salary seems to have remained at that level for the rest of the 17th century, but it is to be understood that the deputy constable might still continue to draw special fees, in addition to this fixed salary, if he held other paid offices concurrently. Robert Haulgh, who was appointed deputy constable in 1669, was at the same time appointed catchpole and appraiser, and held all three offices until his death in 1674; Charles Platt then succeeded him in the same three offices.[8]

The early Constables of Manchester must have led a very harassed life, in spite of the help they received. Even in normal years the constables lot was not a happy one, while in times of pestilence or civil warfare it was almost impossible to find any responsible person who would accept the office. In the plague years at the beginning of the 17th century disputes about the election of constables threatened the 'peace and quiet' government of Manchester, so seriously that the Crown had to intervene. Anthony Mosley and Adam Smith, who were elected constables in 1603, flatly refused to serve and had to be replaced. More serious trouble arose in the succeeding year, when Robert Robinson refused the office and was fined £3. 6. 8d; the jury in addition to fining him, also reaffirmed his appointment, saying that they elected Robert Robinson to the said office, and that they would elect nobody else. This caused a complete deadlock, which was only ended by the issue of a King's Mandate to the Sheriff of Lancashire, and to the High Constable of the hundred of Salford, ordering them to see that the oath of office was administered to John Bowker, a Manchester haberdasher.[9]

Even in quieter times the constables had an embarrassing variety of functions to perform, or at least to supervise; their financial responsibilities were considerable, and the system of paying fees and expenses for particular services must have complicated the work enormously. The constables were not only responsible for the regular payment of wages or fees to such officials as the catchpole, beadle, and deputy constable, but they had also to make a continual stream of disbursements, large or small, for such miscellaneous services as "beating the drum two days at the General Muster;" Walking through the town two days at Whitsuntide;" "punishing Margaret Buckley for troubling market folk in the meal house;" "conveying out of town one James Smith, a leper;" "watching the town when the Cheshire soldiers were here two nights." There were also "rogues, vagabonds and sturdy beggars" to be whipped, relieved and sent out of town; soldiers to be billetted; 'racusants' to be presented; scolding women to be cucked (ducked); plague victims to be isolated at the Collyhurst cabins; judges banquets to be provided and paid for; each of these occasions requiring a separate entry in the constables account book.

The following is an extract from a page in the accounts ledger of 1758. It is interesting to note that it had become customary to commemorate certain days in the year — such as anniversaries of the King's Birthday, of the Gunpowder Plot, of the Restoration of Charles II — by bonfires and by banquets in the town, on which comparatively large sums of money were spent:

NOVEMBER 5   To a bonfire on the King's Coronation
and another on powder plot: 12s 0d

To cleansing the Lamps at
Cross and Dungeon: 2s 6d

To writing and returning a present'n
(assessment or ley) to the last
Quarter Sessions: 1s 0d

To deputy's expenses attending same: 2s 0d

NOVEMBER 9   To three vagrants to Kendale: 1s 0d

NOVEMBER 10 To Boonfire, his Majesty's Birthday: 6s 0d

To music and wine, drinking the
Royal healths: £2 16s 0d

NOVEMBER 11 To playing and cleansing the
Engines last month 10/-, Ale 6d   10s 6d

To sundry vagrants and passengers: 2s 6d

To High Constable's warrant the wages
of the Governor of the House of
Correction: £2 9s 0d

To more maintenance for Esther
Partington* kept till now in custody: 5s 6d

To the women keeping her in custody
for a month and three days: 15s 6d

To messenger, horse hire, and other
incident charges attending and
conveying her to Lancaster Castle: £2 15s 0d

NOVEMBER 15 To sundry expenses: 3s 6d

To apprehending, attending
committing and conveying Bet. Barratt

> a notorious whore to the House of
> Correction: 4s 0d

Re: *ESTHER PARTINGTON*

On October 17th 1758, the following report appeared in the Manchester Mercury: "Last week, a woman at Shudehill delivered herself of a child in the night-time, which it is said she immediately destroyed. Proper care is taken of her." Later reports indicate that Esther Partington was tried at the March Assizes at Lancaster and convicted of murder, but she was subsequently reprieved from execution. What became of this poor woman is not known.

The "commemorate banquets" and "boonfires" attracted large numbers of travellers, vagrants and thieves to Manchester. During such periods the deputy constable and beadles were supplimented by the casual employment of warders and patrols. Thus, we find in 1761 four warders employed "to prevent throwing at cocks on Shrove Monday," and eleven years later, five warders paid for "clearing the streets of Manchester, it being suspected the town was full of thieves and pick-pockets."[10]

It is tempting to speculate as to the character and status of such casual warders in relation to the later history of the day police.

The fact that the 17th century warders were sometimes paid for "searching and spying" may suggest that they developed later into the professional informers and agent provocateurs who discovered so many mare's nests during Joseph Nadin's reign as deputy constable. The Manchester constables were certainly making payments for "Informations" throughout the later 18th century.[11] However, the likliest professional descendants of the early warders were probably the "Street-keepers" who, in the second quarter of the 19th century formed the lowest grade of the day police in Manchester, ranking below the beadles and their assistants. Clearly it would be misleading to describe the early warders and patrols as direct professional ancestors of the modern policeman; but it becomes evident that throughout the 17th century and 18th century, the constables of Manchester could always command the services of this group of professional hangers-on to supplement the more official efforts of the successive deputy constables and beadles.

Meanwhile the professional standing of the deputy constables and beadles did not remain unchanged during the two centuries which preceded the incorporation of the borough. The beadle, who in the reign of Elizabeth seems to have been an unpaid officer, intermittently appointed and receiving merely occasional fees for special services, had by the later 17th century, become a regularly appointed officer of the Court Leet, with a fixed wage of "two shillings a week and no more" in addition to his gown of office.[12] In 1734 the constables were authorised to increase the customary wages by forty shillings a year, if they thought that the beadle deserved the rise, and this discretionary advance soon led to the beadles receiving the higher salary of 'seven pounds for the year'. By the early years of George III's reign the salary had been further increased to £10.00 per year, and the beadle's uniform was becoming even more resplendent than it had been in the previous century. He was now provided not only with cap and gown, whip and staff, but also with shoes and stockings; the stockings were scarlet, and the cap was decorated with gold lace and a tassel. Presumably he left his gorgeous uniform at home when he cleaned the dungeon, for which he was paid sixpence a time (with eightpence extra for fresh straw).

During the generation of rebellion and warfare against France between the years 1789 and 1815, various changes took place in the number and salaries of the beadles, including the temporary appointment of a head beadle at £60.00 a year to work with two junior beadles at £20.00 each; but before the end of the wars it had become the general rule to appoint four beadles, each receiving the same salary and all equally subordinate to the deputy constable. In 1829, the deputy constable seems to have under his command four beadles, seven assistants, and four street-keepers reinforced on extraordinary occasions by about two hundred special constables, whose main qualification for police work was the possession of an official truncheon; this day police force was expected to control a growing and sometimes turbulent population of more than 150,000 persons.

In such difficult circumstances, whether the professional day police force was to be tolerably efficient or merely futile would largely depend on the character and energy of the deputy constable. Originally the deputy constable's office had been not much better paid than that of the beadle; the beadle's weekly wage had, indeed, amounted to more than the "salary" of the deputy constable, though the latter received more in occasional fees, some of which were very hardly earned. In the first quarter of the 17th century the deputy constable was paid (apart from occasional fees) only £1. a year, while the beadle's weekly wages amounted to £2 12s 0d a year. By the end of the 17th century this apparent anomaly had been remedied; the deputy constable now got a fixed salary of £10. a year, while the beadle received only two shillings a week. Even so, the deputy constable may have been relatively underpaid, considering the greater responsibilities which he had to shoulder; there is no recorded instance of a beadle refusing to continue in office, but Benjamin Bowker, who was elected deputy constable in 1734, flatly refused to accept re-appointment in 1736, and was fined £5 0 0d for contempt of court.[13] He was eventually induced to continue, and held the office until 1749, but it is clear that he did not regard the job as a sinecure. His position may have been especially difficult during the Jacobite Rebellion of 1745 when the Young Pretender and his forces twice passed through Manchester; no doubt the jury of the Court Leet had the political situation in mind when they raised the deputy constable's salary from £10 to £20 in October 1745. Thenceforward the emoluments of the office increased rapidly, to £30 a year in 1762, £80 in 1778, and in 1786 to £150, at which amount it remained fixed for nearly twenty years, a generation of almost incessant unrest.

The deputy constable could hardly escape condemnation at such a time when local civil and religious dissention was aggravated by the war-time hatred of "Jacobinism" and the threat of French invasion; but Richard Unite, who became deputy constable in 1792 seems to have deserved most of the obloquy which was cast upon him. Within a few months of his appointment he played a most discreditable part in the "Church and King" riots of December 1792, when the mob smashed up the offices of Faulkner and Birch the printers of the Manchester Herald, a local paper which advocated a reform of parliament in the belief that such measures constituted support for a French system of democracy. Having thus demonstrated his loyalty to the dominant party in the town, Mr. Unite soon became salaried overseer of the poor as well as deputy constable, and during the next few years he feathered his nest very energetically by flagrantly corrupt practices. The duty of billeting soldiers upon the innkeepers of the township was turned into a lucrative source of private revenue. In order to be favoured in the distribution of billets, each innkeeper was induced to make a series of presents to the all-powerful official. Thieves and the persons from whom they had stolen were alike laid under contribution, stolen property being impounded, and in many cases converted to private uses. The poor were paid their weekly allowance in base and counterfeit copper coin, while the threat of bastardy proceedings gave ample opportunity for private blackmail and the taking of hush money. Finally, this ingenious official, contriving so to use his various powers that each should yield him profit, would at any time oblige a friend or subscriber by apprehending any troublesome person as a vagrant, or by locking up a troublesome wife as a lunatic.[14]

This pace was too hot to last long. In 1794 the parochial authorities had to make two successive rates of five shillings in the pound, and the ratepayers were stung to protest. The parish and township officers were accused of ignorance, mismanagement, peculation, and breach of trust. A public meeting, called according to custom by the boroughreeve and constables, elected a committee of twelve to investigate the activities of the deputy constable. The enquiry revealed that the local administration of Manchester had become shockingly corrupt, and the main blame was justifiably thrown upon Unite. He hung on to the office of deputy constable until 1796, and was then superceded by one Thomas Slack who had previously kept a grocer's shop at the top of Market Street Lane. Unfortunately Slack was drowned at Liverpool only a few weeks after his appointment; he was executing the duties of his office by conducting a batch of naval "volunteers" to the frigate Actacon when the boat overturned and most of the party were drowned. Unite seized the opportunity to usurp the office of deputy constable once again, but the Court Leet nipped this piratical scheme in the bud. In advertising for "an honest, sober, industrious and active person to serve the office of Deputy Constable," they announced that "no person needs to apply whose character will not bear the strictest enquiry." The advertisement carried an addendum, "to prevent any misunderstanding, Richard Unite who last Saturday called himself deputy constable has not been appointed to that office." The disclaimer was effective, and the name of Unite did not appear in the records of the Manchester Court Leet after this date.

Eventually the office was filled by the appointment of William Waters, who held the office without scandal until 1802, when he was succeeded by Joseph Nadin, the most notorious of all Manchester's deputy constables.

Born in 1765, Nadin began life as a spinner before finding his metier as a policeman, eighteenth century version. From the start he was a renowned thief-catcher with the reputation for turning every offence into a felony. The significance of this peculiar twist is that a successful felonious charge was rewarded with a fee of 40s, plus a Tyburn ticket. The Tyburn Ticket Acts of 1699 and 1706 exempted the holder from any public office in the town. Possession of a ticket freed a man from the irksome office of constable or from the charge of hiring a substitute and they changed hands at high prices. "Tyburn Tickets" frequently being advertised for sale by public auction.

Between 1800 and 1819 the selling price for Tyburn tickets among the "public-spirited citizens of Manchester" was 300s to 400s. From his frequent sales Joseph Nadin amassed a small fortune.

During his early years in office Nadin was also appointed to several other offices under the Court Leet; by 1806 he was a 'market looker for fish and flesh,' an officer for corn weights and measures, and also an officer to prevent ingrossing, regrating, and forestalling,* and he continued in those offices for many years without intermission.[15]

He had plenty of opportunities for feathering his own nest, and he may have used some of them, as was the general custom of the times, but he never lost the confidence of the local authorities as did Richard Unite.

Samuel Bamford, the Middleton radical poet-weaver, recalls the first occasion he was arrested by Joseph Nadin. The date was the 29th of March 1817, "I was walking towards the Churchyard, when a voice hallooed, and looking back I beheld

*Corrupt practices by corn dealers to inflate the market place.

Joseph Scott, the deputy constable of Middleton, hastening towards me. I concluded instantly that he wanted me; and disdaining the thought of flying, I returned and met him, and he took hold of me, saying I was the King's prisoner. I asked him what for? and he said I should see presently; and we had not gone many yards on our return when we were met by Mr. Nadin the deputy constable of Manchester, and about six or eight police officers, all well armed with staves, pistols, and blunder busses . . . Nadin was, I should suppose, about 6 feet 1 inch in height with an uncommon breadth and solidity of frame. He was also as well as he was strongly built, upright in gait and active in motion. His head was full sized, his complexion sallow, his hair dark and slightly grey; his features were broad and non-intellectual, his voice loud, his language coarse and illiterate, and his manner rude and overbearing to equals or inferiors. He was represented as being exceedingly crafty in his business, and somewhat unfeeling withal; but I never heard, and certainly never knew that he maltreated his prisoners. At times he would indulge in a little raillery with them, possibly for a reason of his own, but I never was led to suppose that he threw away a word of condolement on those occasions. He was certainly a somewhat remarkable person in uncommon times, and acting in an arduous situation. He showed, however, that he had the homely tact to take care of his own interests. He housed a good harvest whilst his sun was up, and retired to spend his evening in ease and plenty on a farm of his own within the borders of Cheshire."[16]

That the Court Leet valued his services very highly may be gathered from the rapidity with which his salary as deputy constable increased, from £150 a year on his first appointment to £200 in 1805, £300 in 1807, and finally to £350 in 1810.

It was not only the Court Leet which came to admire the talents of Joseph Nadin. In 1805 Manchester's Police Commissioners, established by statute in 1792 with powers to cleanse, watch, light and regulate the streets, requested Nadin to assume the superintendence of the night watch under their control. The commissioners had superseded the Court Leet in the control of most of the public services, but it must be confessed that the immediate results of this transference of control were not very promising. It might be argued that by asking Nadin to take over the superintendence of the night watchmen, in addition to his command of the day police, they were really acknowledging the partial failure of the new system; for the superintendence of the night watchmen had been part of the ordinary duties of the deputy constable until it was taken out of the hands of the Court Leet under the act of 1792.

Manchester's night watchmen had for many years been subjected to severe, and often justifiable criticism from the townspeople. In 1578, the jury of the Court Leet complained about negligence and dishonesty of "wicked watchmen who have been hired or rather bribed with money." For the prevention of such abuses the jury issued an order warning the constables that they should "take none to the watch but such as are known to be honest, discreet, and sober men, being able to yield account of the living, favourers to virtue and enemies to vice, no persons of misbehaviour, no suspected persons, no persons heretofore with bribes corrupted, nor any such like."[17] Apparently this warning wasn't heeded because in 1610, the jury ordered that if any person appointed to serve as a watchman sent an 'insufficient' person as his substitute, the offender should be compelled to serve in person, or else to pay a fine of 6s 8d; from this it was, but a short step to the engagement of public watchmen paid out of the local rates.

The period of watching varied slightly from year to year, but there was a general tendency to employ the night watchmen from Martinmas until Candlemas, that is from the 11th November until the 2nd February. It had long been customary to provide candles for watchman's lanterns "in the dark nights when it was not moonshine."[18] In 1653 the constables were ordered to provide also "a hand bell, which said bell shall every night be carried and used by the watch, who shall at every hour's end in their walking about the town give notice to the inhabitants of their vigilance by ringing the bell." Thenceforward the Manchester night watchmen are clearly recognisable as the professional ancestors of those local "old charlies" who kept Thomas Carlyle awake with their rattles and their hourly cries when he visited Manchester in 1838.

The annual appointment of two watchmen was apparently beginning to be considered an inadequate provision for the nightly protection of Manchester even before the end of the

17th century, such conflagrations as the Great Fire of London may well have aroused fears of a similar catastrophe in Manchester, where brick buildings were still rare. In 1677, the jury ordered that every inhabitant should, according to his turn and time, either watch himself or appoint some sufficient person to do his duty. But for how long this experiment lasted cannot be ascertained because of the destruction or loss of the Court Leet records of the period 1687–1731.

The local unrest accompanying the Jacobite Rebellion of 1745 exposed the inadequacy of both the day police and the night watch. The maintenance of a "privy watch" in August 1745, may indicate that the constables were already anxious about the strength of the local Jacobite faction; by the middle of September there was already talk of the Pretender coming and, early in October, General Cholmondeley "marched into town with 1700 soldiers going against the rebellion in the north."[19] Soon the constables were paying for new handcuffs and for the repairing of the watchmen's billhooks. It was at this time, too that a regular watch-house was established with a coal fire. On several occasions during the critical month of November, the Manchester Constables had to hire additional watchmen, at 8d a night, for Redbank and Newton Lane districts to stop the mob coming into town, and by December, a cordon of watchmen was established "on Salford Bridge and all other ends of town to prevent any intelligence following the rebels of his Royal Highness's army being in close pursuit."[20]

The ordinary night watchmen, even when they got their billhooks repaired, seemed quite unable to cope with the emergency. From that time onwards there was almost continuous grumbling about the inadequacy of the night watch, and several schemes for its reformation were promoted during the second half of the century, prior to the Act of 1792.

The watchman's rounds were regulated according to a set routine. Every evening before going on their rounds all the watchmen were to assemble at the watch office to be inspected as to cleanliness, sobriety, and general fitness for duty. They then reported to their respective corporals and were given a lantern, a rick and a padlock, before going out on their beats.

Lanterns were a most essential piece of equipment for the lonely watchmen. During the 18th century the streets of

Manchester were illuminated solely by two oil lamps, one on the old bridge across the Irwell and the other at the Manchester Cross. It was in 1807 that the Manchester Commissioners installed the first gas burner in the town above the Central Police Office, in Police Street, Deansgate. The succeeding decades saw a fairly rapid expansion of gas lighting in the main thoroughfares of the town. By 1826, four and threequarter miles of streets were illuminated by gas lamps and burners.

The padlock served to secure premises that were found unlocked. If the watchman found it necessary to get in touch with other watchmen he would "spring his rick," or rattle. He was also expected to reassure the townspeople that all was well with his hourly call of the time of the night. In the early hours of the morning he would perform a social service by "knocking-up" the mill workers starting work at 6.0 o'clock..

At this time all warehouses and banks closed from 1.00 p.m. until 2.00 p.m. every working day and all the staff walked home for dinner leaving the district virtually deserted. This practice would seem peculiar to Manchester, for it is reported that visiting merchants and bankers were astounded by it. Streets were so quiet at this hour that several robberies took place, for even the old paupers who acted as watchmen were asleep in their beds and the day police were so few in number. The protection afforded to these properties and their staff was so inefficient that the occupiers subscribed together and appointed private watchmen to look after their warehouses etc. – not only during the night but also in the dinner hour.[21]

Fifty three watchmen were employed in Manchester by 1815, each working a ten hour shift starting at 8 o'clock at night and ending at 6 o'clock the following morning. By 1825 this number had increased to seventy four and their wages varied between thirteen and eighteen shillings per week. By this time the night watch contained three recognised ranks; constable, corporal and sergeant, and each watchman was issued with personalised numbers which they wore on their uniforms for identification.

Theirs was a thankless task, subjected to vile abuse from the community at large, attacked and beaten-up by the street walkers and depredators, with little remuneration at the week's end, they often as not retreated to their boxes after midnight turning out occasionally if they happened to be awake, to call out the time of the hour.

In 1835, Manchester's Watchmen apprehended no less than 2080 persons; an additional 455 were apprehended by the local citizenry and handed over to the Watchmen. Prisoners were housed prior to their appearance at court in one of six lock-ups in the town. These were sited at: the Town Hall in King Street; Swan Street, Shudehill; Kirby Street, Ancoats; Deansgate: London Road; and Oldham Road.

NOTES - (1) Manchester Constables Accounts 1891, Vol 1,p.8-10. (2) Manchester Court Leet Records Vol.2p.119. (3) Ibid. Vol.1,p.22. (4) Manchester Court Leet Records. Vol.1,p.16-17 (5) Manchester Constables Accounts. Vol.1,p.30-6. (6) Ibid.p.120 etc. (7) Manchester Court Leet Records, Vol.4.p.25. (8) Ibid. Vol.5 pp.89,91,216. (9) Ibid. Vol.2,p.205-7. (10) Manchester Constables Accounts, Vol.3,pp.132 and 245. (11) Ibid. Vol.3,p.64. (12) Manchester Court Leet Records, Vol.5.p.187 (13) Ibid. Vol.7, p.35,55. (14) S. & B. Webb. The Parish and the County. P.75-76. (15) Manchester Court Leet Records, Vol.9 pp.192, 201, 210. (16) Samuel Bamford, Passages in the Life of a Radical, p.74-75. (17) Manchester Court Leet Records. Vol.1, p.195. (18) Manchester Constables Accounts, Vol.1, p.262. (19) Ibid. Vol.3, p.17. (20) Manchester Court Leet Records Vol.7,p.250. (21) Manchester Examiner and Times, 23/3/1883.

Chapter Two

PETERLOO.

At the beginning of the 19th century, Manchester started to evolve into the modern city as we know it, but it's interesting to note the condition of the township in its embryonic state. King Street for example had only recently been cut through to Deansgate; Piccadilly was a broad space, as it is now, and was then called " the most pleasant situation in the town." The infirmary was on the site, and in front of the Infirmary was a large pond surrounded by iron railings; Mosley Street was the most fashionable residential street in the whole town. The Piccadilly end of Tib Street was called Stable Street, probably because it ran along the back of the Bridgewater Arms Hotel which was the town's principal coaching house. Corporation Street did not exist.

Oxford Street and Lower Mosley Street and all the districts beyond were yet fields and gardens. High Street and Cannon Street and the upper end of Market Street and St. Ann's Square were private dwellings. Between Oldham Road and Rochdale Road, the ground was open, and St. George's Church stood by itself. Bradford Road was marked but not built, Mill Street, then called Hallsworth Street, at the top had only occasional houses. Great Ancoats Street was only built as far as Port Street and Union Street and Ancoats Hall stood alone at the end. [1].

Mr. James Wheeler, a contemporary chronicler, recorded, "The period was now approaching at which Manchester began to be regarded as the centre of widespread and deeply ramified social disorganisation."

With the haunting spectre of Revolution in France uppermost in their minds, the authorities were ever vigilant to suppress outbreaks of public disorder in the town. Invariably this meant calling out the military to supplement the inadequate civil forces of law and order. Ultimately the severity with which the military quelled public gatherings and disturbances prompted several liberal contemporaries to question the utility of maintaining such an inept body of police.

The following is an account of a food riot, and not an infrequent occurrence, which was put down by the intervention of the military. The rioting took place on the 21st April 1812, in Oldham Road, New Cross, when a cart carrying food to the markets at Shudehill was stopped and its load carried off. Shops in the vicinity were also attacked and their contents looted. The mob was eventually dispersed by the soldiers, but only as far as nearby Middleton. There they met up with an assembly of handloom weavers, miners and out of work factory operatives gathered to protest against the introduction of power loom machinery at Burton and Sons weaving mill.

The mob, which had grown 2000 strong, began by throwing stones at the windows of the factory. The authorities' reaction was pre-planned and decisive, and is vividly described by Archibald Prentice in his "Recollections," [2].

> "the internal part of the building being guarded, a musket was discharged in the hope of intimidating and dispersing the assailants but it was found ineffectual, the throwing of stones continuing, and at the expiration of about fifteen minutes, firing of ball commenced from the factory, and in a very short time the effects were too shockingly seen in the death of three and, it is said, about ten wounded. Here this horrid conflict terminated for that night, which was spent in dreadful preparation.
>
> The morning brought with it fearful apprehension; the insurgents again assembled many of them armed with guns, scythes tied to the ends of poles etc., the factory was protected by soldiers, so strongly as to be impregnable; they then flew to the house of Mr. Burton, where they wreaked their vengeance by setting it on fire. A party of soldiers, horse and foot, from Manchester arriving, pursued those misguided people, some of whom made a feeble stand; but here again death was the consequence, five of them being shot and many of them severely wounded."

For many of these Manchester 'Luddites,' it was chronic hunger and under employment which motivated their actions. The notion of revolution received little support. This remained so in 1815 when the protracted wars with Napolean ended, and a further period of economic depression began. It was in this year that a landowning Parliament passed the corn laws protecting growers from the vagaries of the free market by excluding foreign wheat until its price reached 80s., a "famine price level." Manchester, like other manufacturing districts, felt the impoverishing effects of the law. The labouring population not only had to endure the high price of necessaries, but also a further strain on the labour market as thousands of demobbed soldiers and sailors returned from the French wars in search of work.

Towards the close of 1816, the people, disappointed in their expectations that prosperity and plenty would follow in the train of peace, and having no faith in a legislature which, the moment when the war ended, had inflicted the corn laws, demanded a better representation in Parliament.

Demands for a more representative Parliament grew apace. Hampden Clubs, associations of working men in support of Parliamentary reform, were formed in towns and villages around Manchester. Club members met weekly to read political tracts from popular writers like William Cobbett and to listen to the oratory of local reformers like Samuel Bamford and William Ogden.

The authorities soon became suspicious of these secret meetings of working men, and in 1817 the act of Habeus Corpus, which had prohibited detection without trial was suspended by Parliament. In Manchester many individuals suffered under the suspension of the law at the hands of Joseph Nadin.

Old John Knight reported that, on the night of the 30th of March, 1817, he had been apprehended in bed by Nadin, handcuffed, and conveyed to the New Bailey prison, and kept there till the 6th of April, and then sent, heavily ironed, to London, and committed to Tothill-fields prison "on suspicion" of high treason. He was confined until the end of the year and then discharged "impaired in health by long and close imprisonment, and his family and pecuniary affairs incalculably injured." Joseph Mitchell, in like manner, complained of an incarceration of 240 days on a charge of high treason, never attempted to be substantiated. William Ogden stated that he, an old man of 74, had been apprehended by Nadin on the 9th March, 1817, and sent off to Horsemonger Lane prison, where the ponderous irons

31

with which he was loaded "broke his belly," and dangerous hernia ensued. [3].

Believing that the Monarch himself would not be a willing party to these acts of tyranny, thousands of Manchester men set out on the 10th March 1817, to march to London to petition the King. The marchers – known as the 'Blanketeers' – reached Lancashire Hill, near Stockport, before being dispersed by a body of soldiers who had arrived from Manchester. One hundred and sixty seven were taken prisoner and several received sabre wounds. One man was shot dead. Not surprisingly, the forces of law and order were viewed with deep suspicion and contempt by a great majority of Manchester's working population. Such feeling became engrained into the minds of generations of working people following the massacre of reformists at St. Peter's Fields.

In the year 1819, the famous "Peterloo Massacre" took place. Joseph Nadin was still in office as the deputy Constable. The massacre occurred in St. Peter's Field, which at that time lay between Peter Street and Windmill Street.

During the morning of the 16th August marchers from all parts of what is now Greater Manchester, set out from their homes carrying banners, flags and 'caps of liberty' to attend the Reform meeting in the centre of Manchester. It was estimated that between 50,000 and 60,000 people assembled on the field to listen to Mr. Henry 'Orator' Hunt the principal speaker. The gathering had been called to take into consideration "the most speedy and effectual mode of obtaining radical reform in the Commons House of Parliament; and to consider the propriety of the unrepresented inhabitants of Manchester electing a person to represent them in Parliament."

The magistrates assembled at 11.0. a.m. at a house in Mount Street overlooking St. Peter's Field and about 100 yards from the hustings where Hunt and his fellow speakers were to address the crowd. Troops were stationed in various parts of the town; the Manchester and Salford Yeomanry off Portland Street, regulars of the 15th Hussars and Cheshire Yeomanry in St. John Street, and other contingents of regulars in Lower Mosley Street Brazennose Street and Dickinson Street. Between the Magistrates House and the hustings was a double line of special constables numbering about three hundred.

The chief Magistrate, Mr. William Hulton formed the opinion

that the town was "in great danger," and ordered Nadin to arrest the leaders. Nadin declared that the three hundred men at his disposal were not a sufficient force to enable him to execute the warrant, whereupon messengers were sent to Portland Street for the Yeomanry and to St. John Street for the Hussars and the Cheshires.

The Reverend Edward Stanley, Rector of Alderley, an eye-witness, described the scene:

"As the cavalry approached the dense mass of people, they used their utmost efforts to escape; but so closely were they pressed in opposite directions by the soldiers, the special constables, the position of the hustings, and their own numbers that immediate escape was impossible. On their arrival at the hustings a scene of dreadful confusion ensued. (The 15th Hussars) then pressed forward, crossing the avenue of constables, which opened to let them through, and bent their course towards the Manchester Yeomanry. The people were in a state of utter rout and confusion, leaving the ground strewn with hats and shoes, hundreds were thrown down in the attempt to escape. The cavalry were hurrying about in all directions, completing the work of dispersion, which was effected in so short a space of time to appear as if done by magic. During the whole of this confusion, heightened at its close by the rattle of some artillery crossing the square, shrieks were heard in all directions, and as the crowd of people dispersed the effects of the conflict became visible. Some were seen bleeding on the ground and unable to rise; others, less severely injured but faint with the loss of blood were retiring slowly or leaning upon the others for support. The whole of this extraordinary scene was the work of a few minutes."

Samual Bamford recalled the scene after the havoc,

"the field was an open and almost deserted space. The sun looked down through a sultry and motionless air; the curtains and blinds of the windows, within view, were all closed. The hustings remained, with a few broken and hewed flag-staves erect, and a torn or gashed banner or two drooping, whilst over the whole field were strewed caps, bonnets, hats, shawls, and shoes, and other male and female dress, trampled, torn, and bloody. The yeomanry had

dismounted; some easing their horses girths, others adjusting their accoutrements, and some were wiping their sabres. Several mounds of human beings still remained where they had fallen, crushed down and smothered; some of these were still groaning; others, with staring eyes, were gasping for breath; and others would never breath anymore. All were silent save those low sounds, and the occasional snorting and pawing of steeds."

Eleven persons were killed and at least six hundred wounded. One of those killed was a special constable named John Ashworth who was crushed to death in the chaos round the hustings. The list of those killed at Peterloo is as follows:

John Ashton, Cowhill, Oldham; sabred.

John Ashworth, of the Bull's Head, Manchester; sabred and tramped on.

Thomas Buckley, Baretrees, Chadderton; sabred and stabbed.

William Dawson, Saddleworth; crushed and sabred.

John Lees, Oldham; sabred.

William Fildes, Kennedy Street, Manchester, a 2 year old infant rode over by the cavalry.

Arthur O'Neill, Pigeon Street, Manchester; inwardly crushed.

Martha Partington, Eccles; thrown into a cellar and killed.

Joseph Whitworth, Hyde; shot.

James Crompton, Barton; trampled on.

Mary Heys, Oxford Street, Manchester; ridden over by the cavalry.

For the remainder of that fateful August day the military joined forces with the local police in patrolling the township's streets and troublespots. By early evening a large crowd had gathered at New Cross, a popular meeting place for the residents of Ancoats and Collyhurst. Very soon a few of the more unruly elements among them started throwing stones at the patrolling soldiers. The officer in command responded by ordering his men to open fire. Within minutes the crowd had dispersed, one man, Joseph Ashworth, lay dead and several others lay injured.

Despite the cruelty of the authorities, there was no wild revenge for the injuries received. Archibald Prentice wrote, "In that paralysis of terror, anything might have been done. But the men and women of South Lancashire would not seek reform through the horrors of a sanguinary revolution."

Nadin retired from office soon after the events at Peterloo and took to farming in the Cheshire countryside. A peaceful end to a profitable career.

His successor was a former Bow Street runner named Joseph Lavender who resided in a house in King Street, on the site where the Bank of England Building stands today.

Lavender's staff included four beadles, whose names were Thomas Worthington, George Moss, Anthony Jefferson and John Page; seven assistants and four street-keepers. "The colour of their livery was brown," recalled J. T. Slugg in his reminiscences of Manchester.

> "I well remember hearing of a riot in the neighbourhood of Ancoats, when one or two factories were set on fire. I was passing the Royal Hotel just as Lavender was coming up Mosley Street at the head of about nine or ten beadles (the writer apparently mistoook the beadle's assistants for beadles) walking in single file, each carrying a drawn cutlass in his hand, and remember seeing them cross over Mosley Street. They were assisted in quelling the disturbance by a number of special constables from the Ancoats district."[4]

A considerable number of Special Constables were sworn annually and made a valuable contribution to the conservation of the peace. We are not told that they did regular duty, but rather that they were called upon to assist the beadles during serious outbreak of disorder. In February, 1823, for instance, the peaceful neighbourhood of Kersal Moor had been for several Sundays "disturbed by large assemblies of persons who met for the purpose of fighting dogs and settling alehouse disputes. The Special Constables of Strangeways turned out but were driven off the ground by a volley of stones. Returning to the charge, with the assistance of the Beadles, they finally dispersed the crowd, though not without injuries to several of their number."

Thus, Manchester in early 19th century, was policed by a hotch-potch of local officials and helpers, none of whom appeared to be above corruption and all of them resorting to brute force and an assortment of weaponry in order to maintain the peace. For those unfortunate depredators who happened to be apprehended and convicted of wrongful acts, there was an assortment of punishments and corrections all designed to deter the wrongdoer from repeating his misdeeds. The fact that so many continued in their old ways after receiving punishments puzzled many contemparies, just as much as the problem of recidivism does today.

NOTES - (1) Manchester City News, 14/4/1902. (2) A. Prentice, Historical Sketches and Personal Recollections of Manchester. (3) Ibid. P.127. (4) J.T.Slugg, Reminiscences of Manchester fifty years ago, p.236.

Chapter Three

Punishments and Corrections.

The inadequacy of the machinery to apprehend criminals brought about a policy of almost mindless repression.

In the Manchester of the 18th and early 19th centuries wrongdoers were punished by imprisonment in the House of Correction, or in the Dungeon on the "Old Bridge;" by public whipping at the Rogue's Post; by leading them in the Scold's Bridle; or by confining them for an indefinite period in the stocks, or the pillory; prostitutes and notorious women were ducked in the public pond by means of the cucking stool.

The cucking stool was first used in Saxon times for the ordeal of putting convicts to death by drowning. The Manchester stool was provided for "scolding women," and women of ill-repute as well as women bakers who sold bread under weight. It remained, at least up to 1775, an open bottomed chair placed upon the end of a long pole which was balanced upon a pivot and suspended over a large quantity of water. The stool was referred to in the Court Leet Records as early as the 6th October 1586, and at that time was probably used at the moat or pool belonging to the house of a branch of the Radcliffe family. In 1619 an entry in the Court Leet records shows that the stool at the Radcliffe House - Poolfold - was to be disused and the "Horsepool" which extended from the High Street entrance some distance up that street towards Market Stead Lane (Market Street) was to be used in its place.

The last siting of the pool was at a water known as "Daubholes" which was in fact the infirmary pond sited where Piccadilly stands today.

The pillory or neck stocks, stood in the Market Place next to the entrance to Old Millgate till the year 1812 when it was removed. A contempory chronicler wrote,

"Noon, Saturday 1812, being Market Day I saw the last man ever subjected to the punishment of the pillory

standing on a table the object of the jeers and "chaff" of
the country folk who had come into the Market Place.
About the same time I also saw two boatmen in a cart in
Deansgate, somewhere about the site of the present library,
these men had been tapping a brandy cask en-route for
London, they were roped to the triangle in the cart and
received each, fifty strokes from "Nadin's Cat-O-Nine
Tails." [1].

The Dungeon was sited on the "Old Bridge" across the Irwell
linking Salford with Manchester. It consisted of two apartments,
one over the other, and was housed in the middle pier of the
triple-arched bridge. They who were so unfortunate as to be
lodged in the lower dungeon were often in a most perilous
situation from the rise of the river by floods which filled the
miserable habitation with water.

Occupying a space between the Chetham Library Buildings
and Hunt's Bank stood the House of Correction. Built in 1581,
the original house for "the detention of rogues, vagabonds and
sturdy beggars" was known as the New Fleet. References to
subscriptions being taken for the erection of a new house on the
same site are to be found in the Constable's Accounts for the
year 1615-16. "These places" says Blackstone, "were originally
designed for the penal confinement, after conviction, of paupers
refusing to work, and other persons falling under the legal
description of vagrant;" their inmates were supposed to undergo a period of compulsory forced labour in order to instil them
with a desire for hard and honest toil. However, Houses of
Correction, or 'Bridewells' as they were sometimes called, were
embodied into the poor law system at its foundation in 1597,
and from then on they were utilized by the justices both for
their intended purpose and for the disposal of the aged and the
infirm, classified under this new scheme as the 'deserving poor."

The distinction between the House of Correction and the
Gaol gradually vanished, and by the 18th century the justices
were allowed to commit a large number of offenders to either
establishment as they saw fit.

In 1783 a disturbing report was published by Mr. Butterworth
Bayley J.P. who had visited the Hunts Bank House of Correction
in May of that year.

"The apartments were much crowded and extremely dirty

*and offensive, as well as the prisoners; who we think were
very improperly put down in the cells at night whilst the
upper rooms, originally intended as night rooms, were
unoccupied. There is no tap in the House. We found the
greater part of the prisoners quite idle and unemployed,
the rest were spinning candlewick, a very unprofitable sort
of labour."*

The prisoners in the Correction House, by the help of bags,
caps or mugs, let down from their barred windows were almost
constantly employed in soliciting the charity of passers-by by
pleading not only charity and sickness, but innocence of the
crimes of which they were accused. The profits from their bags
were then exchanged for intoxicating liquors which were a
principle source of the keeper's income inside the house.

The year after Bayley's report, 1784, the local magistrates
decided to build a new, modern prison, named The New Bailey;
in Stanley Street, Salford. The first inmates were admitted in
1790 and it is reported that each of the orginal 150 prisoners
had a cell to himself. A new female prison was opened in
Rusholme Road in 1822, as a temporary asylum for such women
as, "having deviated from the paths of virtue are desirous to
abandon their vicious courses and to become qualified by virtue
and industry, for reputable situations." [2].

The House of Correction was later sold to a Mr. Gill, managing
director of the Lancashire Railway Company who ordered that
it be pulled down. On the site was built the Palatine Hotel and
a row of shops.

A great difficulty for a humanitarian of this age must have
been how to devise any form of punitive confinement which
would not have been an improvement on the general standard
of living conditions in most of the districts which housed the
labouring poor of Manchester. Describing the Deansgate district
in central Manchester in 1832, Dr. James Kay/Shuttleworth
wrote.

*"Near the centre of the town, a mass of buildings inhabited
by prostitutes and thieves, is intersected by narrow and
loathsome streets, and close courts defiled with refuse.
These nuisances exist in No. 13 district, on the western
side of Deansgate, and chiefly abound in Wood Street,
Spinning Field, Cumberland Street, Parliament Passage,*

Parliament Street, and Thomson Street. In Parliament Street there is only one privy for three hundred and eighty inhabitants, which is placed in a narrow passage whence its effluvia infest the adjacent houses, and must prove a most fertile source of disease. In this street also, cesspools with open grids have been made close to the doors of the houses, in which disgusting refuse accumilates, and whence its noxious effluvia constantly exhale."

Later in his report Dr. Kay examines the dwellings of the workers in the Little Ireland District, (near what is now Granby Row).

"The upper rooms are with few exceptions, very dirty, and the cellars much worse; all damp and some occasionally overflowed. The cellars consist of two rooms on a floor each nine to ten feet square, some inhabited by ten persons, others by more; in many the people have no beds and keep each other warm by close stowage on shavings, straw etc., a change of linen or clothes is an exception to the common practice. Many of the back rooms where they sleep have no other means of ventiliation than from the front rooms." (3).

Few voices were heard in support of any radical reforms in the penal system, the corner stone of which remained the deterrent qualities of the condemned procession and the hangman's rope, instead of the criminal law being revised or penalties which had been prescribed in former centuries being repealed, there was in fact a tendancy towards increased severity.

At the beginning of the 18th Century, few would have questioned the policy of repression which the extension of capital punishment to so many crimes reflected. Indeed, there appeared in 1701 an anonymous tract, under the forbidding title: 'Hanging Not Punishment Enough for Murderers, Highwaymen and Housebreakers,' an ingenious argument that the more terrible the punishment inflicted on convicted criminals, the greater deterrent it will be. The anonymous author was certainly not alone in holding this opinion, but unfortunately, in spite of the establishment of additional capital crimes, law-breaking continued to increase.

On the accession of George II about fifty offences carried the penalty of death; during the thirty-three years of his reign sixty-three further crimes were added to the list. By the end of the century, according to the Report of the Committee on the Criminal Law, the number had increased to over two hundred.

In one celebrated case in the year 1791, James McNamara was brought to trial at Lancaster, and convicted of a burglary committed by himself and four other men in the house of Mr. Cheetham at the Dog and Partridge public house in Stretford Road, Manchester. The following report appears in Edward Baines's Lancashire.

> *"This robbery was not distinguished by any extraordinary personal violence offered to the family; but the public mind was in a state of alarm, and it was thought that the example of a public execution in the neighbourhood of the town might strike terror into the minds of the midnight marauders, and afford security to the persons and property of the inhabitants. Having been conveyed from Lancaster Castle to the New Bailey Prison, he was taken from thence on Saturday the 11th of September, attended by the Chaplain and a large posse of peace officers, to Kersal Moor, where a gallows had been erected upon one of the eminences. The number of spectators attracted by the novel but awful scene was immense, and, from the situation of the gallows, the inhabitants of all the surrounding country had an opportunity of seeing the apparatus of death, and the victim swinging from the beam."* [4].

It is reported that another malefactor, named George Russel, was executed on Newton Heath 1799 for robbing the bleaching croft of a Mr. Shorrocks near Scotland Bridge.

The inhabitants of Manchester and Salford were alarmed in the year 1817 by the murder of Margaret Marsden, aged 75 years, and Hannah Partington, a young woman, the servants of Mr. Thomas Littlewood, in his dwellinghouse at Pendleton. The murder took place during a burglary in the house when cash, plate and other valuables were stolen. The perpetrators of the crime were James Ashcroft, the elder, James Ashcroft, his son, David Ashcroft, his brother, and William Holden, son-in-law of the elder Ashcroft. The family Ashcroft were all convicted and executed at Lancaster Castle.

From 1820 onward the law itself was made less draconian. Between 1830 and 1840 capital punishment was no longer meted out for many such offences as coining and forgery, horse, sheep, and cattle stealing, larceny in dwelling houses to the value of £5, housebreaking, riot and rape. After 1841, murder was the only offence leading to the execution of the offender. What is more, when hanging for serious crimes was abolished those crimes apparently did not increase in number.

NOTES - (1) A. Darbyshire, A book of Olde Manchester and Salford. (2) E. Baines, A History of Lancashire. Vol.2,p.145. (3) J. Kay, The Moral and Physical Condition of the Working Classes in Manchester. P.35 - 36. (4) E. Baines, A History of Lancashire, Vol.2, p.119.

Chapter Four

FROM TOWNSHIP TO BOROUGH.

By the early 19th century it had become abundantly clear that the chief weaknesses of the Manchester Court Leet and the Manchester Police Commissioners were judicial and financial. Neither the officers of the Court Leet nor those of the Police Commissioners had the powers of the justices of the peace; and the lack of resident magistrates able to understand the special problems of town goverment was a source of great danger to the public welfare of Manchester on many occasions during the late 18th century and early 19th century. The Court Leet's right to impose "towns leys" for general administrative purposes had never been clearly defined and after 1778 the Court could not even raise money for the payment of the day police; though the constables of Manchester never experienced any difficulty, until the second quarter of the 19th century, in getting their accounts paid by the church-wardens out of the poor rate.

The Manchester Police Commissioners had the right to levy rates for the purposes defined in the local acts under which they were incorporated, but such police rates might not exceed eighteenpence in the pound in any one year; the tardiness with which the Police Commissioners developed some of the essential public services of Manchester may have been due to this statutory limitation of the police rates. Most of the townspeople, however, regarded this financial limitation of the police commissioners expenditure as a valuable safeguard, rather than as a constitutional defect; one of the strongest objections to municipal incorporation arose from the fear that a borough council, with power to levy an unlimited borough rate for general administrative purposes, might be far more "extravagant" than the police commissioners had been, in spending the ratepayers money upon improvements in public services.

In most branches of local administration the police commissioners had by 1838 built up a strong position; but there was a fatal weakness in their powers over the local machinery for preserving law and order. The day police was clearly inadequate to its task, but the police commissioners had no power to spend any part of their funds in strengthening it. It is true that the commissioners, under the police act of 1830, had the right to employ a mounted or foot patrol for service by day as well as by night; the exercise of this right would have meant, however, not the strengthening of the day police employed by the Court Leet, but the establishment of a supplementary force under the control of the Police Commissioners.

The relations between the Court Leet and the Police Commissioners were friendly, and there was close coordination in normal times between the day police and the night watch; but there could be no guarantee that this happy arrangement would be maintained indefinitely. To have effected a proper consolidation of the day police and the night watch would have necessitated further legislation, and any Bill for such a purpose would have encountered strong opposition from more than one quarter.

The consolidation of the two police forces was actually proposed by William Neild, as chairman of a committee formed in the later months of 1836 to inquire into the local government of the town. "Instances of riot have occurred," reported the committee, "and considerable damage has been sustained, when the aid of the military has been called in, but which might easily have been suppressed in its origin by the civil power had there been a sufficiently numerous and properly organised police force." The Court Leet appointed the officers of the day police, but their salaries – as we have already noted – had to be paid by the churchwardens and overseers out of the poor rate. "Thus the party who makes the appointment can grant no funds, the party who supplies the funds has no power over the appointment." Equally anomalous was the position of the boroughreeve and constables in relation to the police commissioners; partly by customs and partly by ancient Acts of Parliament, the boroughreeve acted as Treasurer and Chairman of the Police Commissioners, while the senior constable was always elected Chairman of the Watch Committee. "These officers are placed at the head of the Commissioners of Police, and yet the commissioners have no more control over their appointment than the ley payers." [1] . Moreover, neither the day police nor the night watch of Manchester had any authority outside the central township, each of the out townships (Hulme, Chorlton-upon-Medlock, Ardwick, and Cheetham) had its own constables, and each, with the exception of Cheetham, had its own statutory body of police commissioners. The day police in the out-townships were notoriously inefficient; Chorlton-upon-Medlock had apparently no day police at all.

William Romaine Callender, when retiring as a police commissioner for the township of Chorlton in 1838, referred to the case of a ratepayer whose house was 'robbed' and who had called every day from Monday to Friday at the Chorlton police office before he could get the assistance of an officer. Mr. Callender went on, "The watchmen in the neighbourhood of Plymouth Grove were frequently found asleep within the porch of my house, and the departing guests had sometimes to step over these vigilant guardians of the peace. On one occasion the Superintendent found one there, and took away his staff, lantern and hat without awakening him." [2].

Neild's proposal, in favour of such a consolidation of the day and night police as would give Manchester "a sufficiently numerous and properly organised police force" had much to commend it; but it was a Whig scheme, and was voted down by the combined forces of the Tories and the Radicals. The Tory leaders of the police commissioners preferred to rely upon informal agreements with the manorial authorities and with the police commissioners of the neighbouring townships, rather than upon any statutory changes.

The opposition of the "Low Radicals" to Neild's proposals seems to have become confused, in some curious fashion, with their hatred of the new poor law of 1834, which was just then being brought into operation in the northern industrial districts. "The rural police, the new poor law, bastille workhouses, separation of man and wife, starvation diet," were all apparently expected to result from the consolidation of the local police forces. [3]. The more responsible Radical leaders, such as Archibald Prentice, were not willing to agree to any strengthening of the police commissioner's powers unless the voting qualification, and with it some measure of control, was extended to all police ratepayers. By early 1838 James Wroe proposed to the Manchester police commissioners that the power to vote at the election of police commissioners should be extended to "all persons who pay police rates," but consideration of this proposal was postponed, on the motion of James Crossley, a Tory, "until the decision of the Privy Council is obtained with reference to granting a charter of incorporation to the borough of Manchester under the general Municipal Corporations Act."

All over the country, it was assumed that the Parliamentary Reform Act of 1832 must be speedily followed by some comprehensive measure of municipal reform, including the grant of municipal self-government to Manchester, Birmingham, and other large unincorporated towns which had now become parliamentary boroughs.

Under the Parliamentary Reform Act Manchester had become a parliamentary borough returning for the first time two members; the new borough comprised of the townships of Manchester, Ardwick, Bradford, Beswick, Cheetham, Chorlton-Upon-Medlock, Harpurhey, Hulme and Newton. These several townships had an aggregate population of about 187,000 in 1831, but of this number over 142,000, lived in the central township. The creation of this large parliamentary borough inevitably stimulated the movement for local constitutional reform of one kind or another.

The possibility that Manchester was soon to become a municipal borough had begun to affect the policy of the Police Commissioners so early as 1833, and the investigations of the Royal Commission on Municipal Corporations were watched with close interest by all parties in Manchester during the succeeding two years. The Municipal Reform Act introduced in 1835 did not provide directly for the incorporation of such towns as Manchester, but did contain the general provision that "if the inhabitant householders of any town or borough in England and Wales shall petition his Majesty to grant to them a charter of incorporation, it shall be lawful for his Majesty, by any such charter if he shall think fit on the advice of his Privy Council to grant the same, to extend to the inhabitants of any such charter, all the powers and provisions in this Act contained." The exact scope of this provision was not altogether clear, but the local municipal reformers considered that it constituted a sufficient reason for supporting the Bill; a petition in favour of the measure was signed by 22,832 inhabitants of Manchester in a single day, and was taken to London post-haste by Thomas Potter and George Hadfield.

The receipt of the Charter was hailed as a decisive victory by the Whig reformers, who anticipated that the opposition of the Tories and Radicals would now collapse.

"Thus after a struggle of great duration and severity," declared the Manchester Guardian, *"the inhabitants of this important and populous borough have made the first great step towards ridding themselves of the old feudal government under which they have laboured, unsuited as it is to the present circumstances of the borough, and towards obtaining municipal institutions more in accordance with the great and growing importance of the town. That a change was absolutely necessary every man admits, whatever may be his politics, and the real question has been, whether that change would be effected by a charter of incorporation, granted under the general law of the land, and vesting the government of the town in the general body of the ratepayers, or by some undefined and untried tinkerings of the present old and worn out system. Between these two plans, we think, no man who values the principles of popular government can hesitate for a moment."*[4]

The Tory-biased Manchester Courier however, struck a more sinister note by advising the townsmen to take no part in the forthcoming municipal elections. The Police Commissioners, the Churchwardens and the Manorial Officials all denied the authority of the new Borough Council, the struggle for municipal democracy was not yet ended.

Immediately after the Borough Council had been elected, it was announced in some of the local newpapers that "in accordance with the opinions of Sir. F. Pollack, Sir William Follett, and Lawrence Pell esq., council learned in the law, the validity of the Charter granted to Manchester would be contested."

In face of these and other legal opinions to the same effect, the Commissioners considered that they were bound by the police acts to maintain their own night watch, "till they are satisfied that the responsibility has been legally removed from them to some other public body, which has undoubted means for effectually and permanently maintaining a proper force. It is currently reported that the Town Council have no funds to cover their expenses but what are derived from voluntary contributions. These contributions may fail any week. The charter may be overturned in the Courts of Law, and in either case the town would be left without protection, if the Commissioners of Police had previously abandoned the force under their government." [5] .

The parochial and manorial authorities adopted the same attitude, and the administration of the town was in danger of being reduced to chaos. In the township of Manchester, the authority of the Borough Watch Committee was denied, both by the constables and by the commissioners of police. The day constables and the watchmen still continued to act − their wages were illegally paid out of the poor's rate and police rate. The parties in possession of the lock-ups and other premises, also of the arms and accoutrements belonging to the town, refused to deliver up the possession thereof. Proceedings were taken to enforce the authority of the Council, and to compel the delivering up of the premises and articles, with results similar to those reached on the rating question. Fines were imposed by the Magistrates, but were not paid. Warrants of distress were issued, and distress was levied for the amount of the fines; in reply, actions were instituted against the Borough Justices who had signed the warrants of distress. This legal conflict was not only a great waste of public money, but also endangered the peace of the borough through the simultaneous operation of "two opposing and counter-acting forces," each claiming to be responsible for the preservation of law and order. [6] .

To make matters worse, the activities of the Chartists were now arousing fears of a general insurrection, in which Manchester would probably be involved, while the agitation for the repeal of the Corn Laws increased the danger of social disturbances such as had been experienced between 1817 and 1819. In a belated attempt to meet this emergency, and to vindicate their position as the main governing authority in the town, the police commissioners attempted to use the extended powers which they had obtained in 1830, for the employment of a "Mounted or Foot Patrol," for service by day as well as by night. In May, 1839, the Watch and Hackney Coach Committee of the commissioners was authorised to appoint any number of patrolmen, not exceeding 50, "and to furnish the necessary arms and appointments." In the circumstances, however, this special reinforcement of the watch served rather to aggravate the conflict of authorities than to preserve the peace. Eventually the Government was obliged to intervene in the dispute, and to take the control of the Manchester police forces out of the hands of the local authorities. A special bill was introduced in the summer of 1839, empowering the Crown to appoint a Chief Commissioner of Police for the borough of Manchester, and to establish a new police office there. The Chief Commissioner was to hold office for two years "and from thence until the end of the then next session of Parliament;" by that time it was hoped that litigation concerning the municipal charter would be at an end. In the meantime, the Chief Commissioner was to be in command of a specially organised police force for the whole borough, and all other police forces were to be disbanded. The various townships were not to levy any watch rates during the Chief Commissioner's term of office, and he was to be authorised to levy a special police rate of not more than eight pence in the pound.

None of the local administrative bodies in Manchester liked this scheme, but they had to acquiesce in it. A deputation sent to London by the Borough Council came reluctantly to the conclusion that the Government's scheme offered the best way of escape from an intolerable situation; "an active opposition was made to the Bill," they concluded, "which, if successful, would have left this great town exposed to the risk of being without any police force adequate to its protection." [8]. The other local authorities were harder to convince. The church-wardens of the parish were authorised by a meeting of rate-payers to cooperate with the boroughreeve and constables, and with the watch committee of the police commissioners in opposing "the Bill for the establishment of a police force which shall not be placed under the direction and control of the boroughreeve and constables and the said committee, or under such regulations as shall be satisfactory to those bodies." [9].

The police commissioners made a valiant attempt at defending their position in a printed circular which was distributed among the members of both Houses of Parliament; they maintained "that the appointment of any individual to take command of the police force in Manchester is wholly unnecessary, as the powers they already possess are fully adequate to every emergency, and have always hitherto been found abundantly sufficient for the preservation of the public peace of the town; than which no town in the Empire has been better conducted and governed up to the present time." A deputation from the police commissioners interviewed Lord John Russell but failed to convince him that these proud boasts were justified. Finally, the deputation were themselves converted to the principle of the Bill by the Duke of Wellington. In all the circumstances, the deputation felt that they "could not resist the high and constitutional principles which actuated the Duke and his Noble Friends;" the Bill passed, and Sir Charles Shaw was appointed Chief Commissioner of Police in the Borough of Manchester. [10]

This temporary solution of the problem was, on the whole, more favourable to the Borough Council than to its opponents. It was a humiliation to the Corporation, but it was even more humiliating to the Court Leet and the Police Commissioners. In particular, it struck a decisive blow at the prestige of the Tory "elders" who were still powerful in the various committees of the commissioners; thenceforward the policy of the commissioners came to be dominated more and more strongly by the Whig municipal reformers, under the leadership of Thomas Potter. Moreover, the government by appointing Sir Charles Shaw to "hold the ring" for two or three years, was giving time for the legal disputes about the charter to be settled; and there could be no doubt that the disputes would eventually lead to the confirmation of the Charter, either by ordinary process of law or by special legislative enactment. The Borough Council could safely assume that the Whig Government, which had granted the Charter, would do its best to safeguard the interests of the new Corporation. The Borough Council had much to gain by submitting patiently to the intrusion of the Chief Commissioner, provided that Sir Charles Shaw's police force proved to be reasonably efficient.

NOTES - (1) Manchester Times and Gazette, 7/1/1837.   (2) Manchester Guardian, 24/2/1838.   (3) W.E.A. Axon, Annals of Manchester, p.10.   (4) Manchester Guardian, 27/10/1839.   (5) Proceedings of Police Commissioners, 10/7/1839. (6) Proceedings of the Borough Council, 10/1/1840.   (7) W.E.A. Axon, Annals of Manchester. p.117-118.   (8) Proceedings of the Borough Council, 4/9/1839. (9) Manchester Parish Table Book, 7/7/1839.   (10) Proceedings of the Borough Council, 4/9/1839.

Chapter Five

THE CHIEF COMMISSIONER

The new commissioner's task proved to be quite formidable. Sir Charles's first impressions of Manchester and its police were not favourable. "I found that both Brown and Blue Police gave much attention to certain properties, taking positions for the whole night close to the houses of certain individuals, and I invariably found that the property most carefully may I say exclusively watched, was that of commissioners of police or local authorities, thus forcing one to suspect that the much famed system of self-government was in reality selfish government. In addition to this the streets of the wealthy were much better watched and lighted than those inhabited by the poor. About the same time a policeman on duty in Hulme saw two men fighting in a field opposite the end of Boundary Street. On close inspection the two combatants turned out to be the Chief of the Police force of Chorlton-on-Medlock and an Inspector of nuisances of the same township."[1]

In another report Sir Charles referred to the practice of policemen knocking-up the workpeople in the town. "I found the workpeople of Manchester in the habit of paying sixpence a week each family to the old watch for calling up in the mornings and immediately put a stop to it. Employers however, complained of the interruption to business, requesting a return to the usual custom." Sir Charles consented to allow the police to call up the workpeople at twopence a week provided the masters would deduct the amount from the weekly wages and pay it over to the police fund. Ultimately the police were relieved of their difficulty by a small staff of professional knockers-up who gradually increased in number until they embraced the city and its suburbs.

In many respects the new police force differed under Sir Charles Shaw's command very little from the old order. Most of its members were recruited from among the Constables

51

previously employed by the Manorial Court Leet. Sir Charles also took over a very liberal proportion of the Police Commissioners' Watchmen. The Superintendent of the nightly watch, M.J. Whitty, was made Head Constable and 53 Watchmen engaged as Constables. It is of incidental interest to note that in appointing 4 superintendents and 24 Inspectors, it was hoped that they would be "so removed in point of class" to avoid "undue familiarity with the constables."[2]

The continuance of these same individuals who had been labelled so inefficient, is not really surprising however On paper the police force was new, but who else but the serving Constables and Watchmen had the experience, and the desire, to work long hours in dangerous and thankless conditions, for often less than fourteen shillings weekly wage.

"RETURN OF THE TOTAL AMOUNT OF THE POLICE FORCE ESTABLISHMENT IN THE BOROUGH OF MANCHESTER DISTINGUISHING THE SEVERAL RANKS AND NUMBERS THEREOF, AND THE PAY AND ALLOWANCES OF EACH RANK."

1	Chief Commissioner	per annum	£700 0s 0d
1	Receiver	,, ,,	£250 0s 0d
1	Chief Clerk	,, ,,	£200 0s 0d
1	Surgeon	,, ,,	£50 0s 0d
1	Chief Superintendent	,, ,,	£260 0s 0d
4	Superintendents, each	,, ,,	£180 0s 0d
8	Inspectors, each	,, ,,	£100 0s 0d
4	Sub-Inspectors	per week	£1 10s 0d
13	Superiors Sergeants	,, ,,	£1 5s 0d
31	Sergeants	,, ,,	£1 1s 0d
295	Constables	,, ,,	17s 0d

The above is the average number of constables and officers for the six months commencing on the 17th October 1839 and ending 17th April 1840.

CHARLES SHAW
CHIEF COMMISSIONER

RETURN OF THE TOTAL EXPENSE OF THE FORCE

Ordinary expenses	£	s	d
Pay Lists	8019	5	2
Stable expenses and forage	64	1	4
Stationary and printing	286	6	10
Coals for offices and police stations	90	2	1
Gas lighting	140	3	3
The Surgeon; for inspecting the constables and medicine	35	16	0
Rent of offices and police stations	210	7	4
Salaries of Chief Commissioner, Receiver, Chief Supt., Chief Clerk, and Superintendent	1103	0	9
Incidental expenses for the offices and all the police stations	273	11	0
	£10,213	13	9

Extraordinary expenses			
Furniture for the offices and stations, and bedding for the constables	558	0	9
Alterations of the offices, stations, lock-ups, and repairs to same	583	8	11
Clothing	2569	14	6
	£3711	3	0

APRIL, 1840

CHARLES SHAW, C.C.
J. THORPE. RECEIVER.

Within a short space of time Sir Charles's force had come under heavy attack. In the summer of 1840 the parochial authorities made Fox Maule's Bill for the more equal assessment of police rates their excuse for a slashing attack on Sir Charles's administration. "The real object of the Bill," they declared, "is manifestly to increase the tax for the maintenance of the police force to a very great and alarming extent. The sum which the Chief Commissioner already receives from the town of Manchester is at least £12,291 per annum, and that exceeds the cost of the day and night police while the management thereof was in the hands of the boroughreeve and constables and the commissioners of Manchester; and the force was then perfectly satisfactory to the public and much more efficient than the force established and conducted by the Chief Commissioner of Police."[3]

In support of their argument the parochial authorities pointed to a recent incident where a large fire had broken out in premises situated in Palace Square. The resultant damage proved to be quite considerable and very expensive. The firm's private watchmen said that they saw a police watchman some time after the fire was discovered, and he told them that he did not know where the fire engines were kept, nor where the police yard was. The police watchman in charge of the district where the fire broke out said that he discovered the fire at about half-past five in the morning and following the instructions given at the police office in such cases, he then went round his beat to give notice of the fire to the other watchmen, but did not communicate it to the Fire Engine Station. If there had been any fireman living in his district, it would have been his duty to call them up, he said, but in fact there was none. The directors of the Manchester Assurance Company which had lost heavily through the fire, declared that the blame for the unnecessary delay must be attributed to the police force rather than the fire engine establishment.

To these charges Sir Charles Shaw replied, in effect, that his police force was not responsible for attending fires, but that when he took up office he had asked Mr. Rose, Superintendent of the Fire Engines, to advise him as to the regulations necessary for the conduct of the watchmen in cases of fire. The regulations proposed were acted upon, and copies were posted in all station houses. The commissioner admitted, however, that the police force under his command was by no means sufficient for the safe protection of the property of the town. This state of things, he said, arose from his inability, under the powers of the Act to raise a sum of money equal to the establishment of a more competent force. In fact, he said, he was even now obliged to reduce its present numerical strength finding the state of his finances insufficient for its support.[4]

Before blaming the Chief Commissioner for his inefficiency, or for his awkwardness when dealing with the conflicting administrative authorities of the district, it is only fair to review the situation from his view point. Even before the end of 1839, he was complaining about "the various and vexatious difficulties which have been thrown in my way since my arrival in Manchester. The results of this opposition," he declared, "have been to circulate reports of every possible nature, calculated to cause either a misapprehension of the measures I from time to time adopted, or to uphold them to public disapproval. Upon my arrival in Manchester, I found three distinct police establishments. The numerical strength of these forces I found to be somewhere near 600 constables, under no general control, and possessing no intercommunity of information, or any unity of action. The sum, however, expended upon these establishments I found to be about £40,000; while, on the contrary, the means at my disposal were £16,502, a sum which, it must be confessed, is obviously inadequate." He had in fact placed himself in a "very responsible situation, by appointing a force so much more numerous than the means at his disposal will warrant." The police force under his command, was still inadequate to the needs of the borough; but it was more effective than it would have been if he had kept strictly within his legal powers.[5]

The Borough Council reported that they fully sympathised with the Chief Commissioner in his difficulties, but they made it quite clear that they would oppose any attempt to extend his tenure of office beyond 1842.

On the 23rd of June of that year Sir James Graham, Home Secretary, brought in a Bill " to amend and continue the Acts regulating the Police of Manchester, Birmingham, and Bolton," whereby it was proposed to extend Sir Charles Shaw's term of office until October 1843. The Manchester Borough Council protested that such an extension was quite unnecessary; the validity of the Charter of incorporation had by 1842 been established by process of law, the various bodies of police commissioners had virtually become executive departments of the Corporation, the overseers of the several townships had ceased to oppose the Borough Council and were now paying the borough rates. After mature consideration, the Home Secretary agreed that it would not be necessary to extend the Police Act beyond the 1st October, 1842, provided that the Borough

Council would give "a distinct pledge that if the existing act be allowed to expire, the council will forth-with take measures for the continuance of an efficient police force so that peace and good order shall not be endangered."

Within weeks of the agreement the "peace and good order" of Manchester was again threatened by working class unrest which created the sort of problems that demanded an efficient and well regulated police. The events of August, 1842, might well have made either the Government or the Borough Council decide to reconsider the question. A threatened reduction of wages resulted in widespread strikes among the Lancashire cotton workers. The disturbances which followed became known as the 'Plug-Plot riots' so called because of the strikers device of knocking out the boiler plugs to immobilize the machinery and so stop the mills from working.

The authorities in Manchester turned to the local militia for protection and it was reported that more than 2,000 soldiers with six pieces of artillery were positioned in the streets alongside the local police.

Additional support was sought from the traditional method of enlisting special constables. The Borough Council reported, "whilst deeply commiserating the distresses under which the working-classes have been for some time past and are now suffering, it is considered to be of the utmost importance that the inhabitants should unequivocally and generally express their disapproval of the illegal and riotous proceeding by which this neighbourhood has been during the last few years disgraced. Aldermen and Councillors of each ward are requested to convene meetings of the respectable inhabitants who are to be urged to come forward for the purpose of being sworn in as special constables."

Mr. Absalom Watkin J.P. a Manchester businessman, described the events of August 10th.

> *"The outrages of the mob continue, those who have been turned out joined with them and shops have been plundered in the town, and money extorted. Message after message arrives for assistance. I am sent with Mr. Stuart and Mr. Higson, to confer with Sir Charles Shaw. We found him at Kennedy's Mill with about 150–200 men, and nearly as many soldiers, taking, as he says, a military view*

of the matter and concentrating his force to be ready to move where it may be urgently wanted: the usual patrols are withdrawn from the streets and all left exposed. He objects to scatter his force. We return. Colonel Weymss objects to scatter the military and refuses to supply us with dragoons for patrol. In the meantime the gasworks (at Gould Street) are attacked and the police stationed there are beaten. A police station in the neighbourhood is pulled down. Mr. Callender goes with some dragoons and rifles, disperses the mob and occupies the gas works in force. While this was going on, the mob proceeded in different parts of the town to turn out the hands at mills and workshops and in some cases to help themselves to bread from the shops. "[6]

Not all contemporaries shared the views of Mr. Watkin and his fellow magistrates. The Manchester Times reported, "The object of the strikers has not been to destroy, but simply to stop, and the simplest and least destructive manner has been chosen. While at a distance Manchester is thought to be in a state of siege, the whole town may be transversed without a single act of violence being witnessed."[7]

Whether 'effective containment' or 'over-reaction' be the case, the Government decided to stand by the agreements made with the Council before the riots had broken out. Sir Charles Shaw's commission was allowed to expire, and on the 1st October 1842, the control and management of the Borough Police Force reverted to the Borough Council. By that time there could be no danger that the Police Commissioners or the Court Leet would attempt to organise rival forces for the preservation of the peace. The Court Leet had ceased to appoint its deputy constable, and beadles — the deputy constable's appointment was last renewed in October 1841 — the Police Commissioners were now in alliance with the Borough Council and had appointed no Watch Committee since 1839. The validity of the Charter of Incorporation had been established beyond cavil, and all responsible parties in the town recognised the authority of the Borough Council.

NOTES - (1) Manchester Guardian, 18/7/1839.   (2) Annual Police Reports, 1839-42 (3) Manchester Parish Table Book, 4/5/1840.   (4) Proceedings of the Manchester Police Commissioners 8/4/1840.   (5) Proceedings of Manchester Borough Council 5/2/1840.   (6) S. Simon, A Century of Local Government, p.331-2. (7) Manchester Times and Examiner, 20/8/1842.

Chapter Six

CAPTAIN EDWARD WILLIS,
THE FIRST CHIEF CONSTABLE.

Manchester's first Chief Constable was Captain Edward Willis. Born in Prescot, Lancashire, in 1806, the youngest of nine sons, Captain Willis received his education at Charterhouse before entering the Army in 1826. He served in this country, Ireland, Bermuda and Jamaica before his retirement in 1837. In 1839 he applied unsuccessfully for appointment as Chief Constable of Lancashire Constabulary, but was offered and accepted the post of Assistant Chief Constable at a salary of £200 per annum. He took over the control and direction, under John Woodford, the Chief Constable, of the southern half of the County with headquarters at Newton-le-Willows.

On the 24th October 1842 he was appointed Chief Constable of Manchester at a salary of £450 per annum with a £50 allowance for expenses. His salary was soon to be increased to £500.

His deputy was Mr. Richard Beswick, former assistant to Sir Charles Shaw and temporary Head Constable between June and October 1842.

The new Chief Constable immediately set about the task of "improving the strength and efficiency of the force," whilst at the same time "endeavouring to introduce the most rigid system of economy."

The minimum wage level for all constables was immediately raised from 14 to 17 shillings per week, which had the effect of attracting seventy additional constables to the force within the first few months.

Despite raising the constables' wage levels, the Chief Constable was able to report a reduction in expenditure to the amount of £585 10s. 2¾d. during his first year in office.

Not surprisingly the ratepayers' representatives were full of praise for their new Chief Constable. "The Watch Committee have deemed it expedient to prepare such a financial statement as will enable the Council to judge how far the advantages usually anticipated, and especially in an economic point of view, from self-government have been realized; and the Watch Committee have much pleasure in directing attention to this part of the Chief Constable's report, as affording strong evidence that the inhabitants of this Borough have good reason to feel satisfied that the management and control of the police has been transferred from the Commissioner appointed by the Crown to the Watch Committee appointed by the Council."

To illustrate the economy of the new force, the Borough Council published the following comparative tables:

i) Manchester Police Force:	Strength:	Pay	Yearly Expense:	Average Cost per Man:
1839 – 1842	328	7s–17s	£23,622	£72.0s. 4½d.
1842 – 1843	398	£0.17s.	£23,036	£57.17s.7½d.

****

ii) Police Forces:	Population of Area	Strength	Gross Cost:	Average Cost per Man:	Cost Per Head of Population
Manchester	235,139	398	£ 23,036	£57.17.7½d	1s.11½d.
City of London	140,967	543	£ 41,351	£76. 3.0d	5s.10d.
Metropolitan	2032,458	4,685	£289,322	£61.15.1d.	2s.10d.

****

Furthermore, according to Captain Willis's report, Manchester was becoming a more peaceful place in which to live. "The borough is generally in an exceedingly orderly and quiet state, and the force have been for some time past, and are now, discharging their duties in a highly creditable and satisfactory manner."

The Chief Constable's observations received a measure of support from Leon Faucher a regular visitor to Manchester, "Public Order in Manchester had advanced; since the establishment of the new police force the streets have been more tranquil, if not more safe, There is no need now, as there was twelve years ago, to engage an extra police force to keep the public roads clear and pick-pockets at a distance, whilst the inhabitants go to and from divine service. A force of three hundred and ninety men under the energetic direction of Mr. Willis and Mr. Beswick suffices to keep the peace and to apprehend delinquents in a town, the population of which exceeds that of Liverpool, a fact which proves that manners are less violent and the inhabitants more occupied."

The following tables taken from the Chief Constable's report for 1843 show the classification of offences and the number of persons apprehended.

OFFENCES AGAINST THE PERSON (1)

MURDER	1
MANSLAUGHTER	11
RAPE	3
INTENT TO COMMIT RAPE	4
BIGAMY	6
CHILD DESERTION	1
ASSAULTS	655
ASSAULTS OF CONSTABLES	417
	1098

OFFENCES AGAINST PROPERTY (2)	Apprehensions
BURGLARY AND ROBBERY WITH VIOLENCE	128
THEFT WITHOUT VIOLENCE	2256
MALICIOUS OFFENCES AGAINST PROPERTY	187
CURRENCY OFFENCES	56
ATTEMPTS AT SUICIDE	11
RIOTING	24
GAMBLING	190
ILLICIT DISTILLATION	33
MISDEMEANORS	305
DRUNKENESS	4198
BREACH OF THE PEACE	725
DESERTION AND NEGLECT OF FAMILIES	141
DISORDERLY PROSTITUTES	836
OTHER VAGRANTS	1869

MISCELLANEOUS OFFENCES   90

Total   12147

Women consitituted a large section of Manchester's criminal population. Of the total 12,147 apprehensions, 3658 were women. Many were engaged in prostitution, often working in concert with pimps and thieves, but not wholly averse to working alone whenever the opportunity presented itself. Robberies and pickpocketing were the commonest forms of crime with which the prostitutes were associated. "Most girls will rob by violence, and especially drunken men," said Ellen Reece an inmate at the Salford Gaol. Prostitutes were also known to practice "picking clients pockets while his trousers were down and then run off while his disarray hampered pursuit." [1]

There were 330 known brothels and 701 common prostitutes in Manchester in 1843. These figures are quite low when compared with those in neighbouring Liverpool which showed 520 brothels and nearly 2,000 prostitutes known to the police in the same year. Leon Faucher suggests a somewhat controversial explanation for Manchester's seemingly low figures, "prostitution for money has little scope amongst the inferior classes where clandestine connexions are so common and where chastity instead of being the rule amongst the females tends to become the exception." [2]

A. B. Reach reporting in 1849 attempted to defend the morality of Manchester's factory girls. "The fact is, as I am assured, that there exists among the mill girls a considerable degree of correct feeling — sometimes, indeed, carried to the extent of a species of saucy prudery — upon these subjects. They keep up a tolerably strict watch upon each other, and a case of frailty is a grand subject for scandal throughout the whole community. There appears, however, to be no doubt whatever that prostitution is rare among the mill girls. In the Manchester Penitentiary in 1847, the number of female inmates who had worked in mills amounted to only one-third of the number who had been domestic servants." [3]

Chronic drunkeness constituted the major threat which constantly undermined the peace, and gave the Manchester Police nearly half of their total work load. Out of a total

12,147 apprehensions for the year, drunkeness accounted for 4,198. Formidable as this figure was, it was not just drunkeness per se which so worried contemporaries but the fact that it led to all manner of crimes and vices, and was the major contributory factor in criminal behaviour. Doctor Hudson reported, "one fifth of all crime in Manchester arises from Drunkeness." [4]. The Reverend Clay, chaplain at Preston Gaol, went even further saying, "I find that at least 35% of all crime must be put down to drinking in beerhouses and public houses." [5].

Manchester's public houses and beerhouses proliferated during this period. In 1843, there were 502 public houses and 781 beerhouses. The beerhouses were licensed to sell beers only, under the terms of the Beer Act 1830. This piece of legislation was a deliberate attempt by the government to wean the working classes away from gin-drinking. It provided that anyone who had a spare room and could afford a few shillings – usually eight – for the licence may lawfully sell beers to the public.

In fact the problem of gin drinking was more prevalent in the large sea ports like London and Liverpool than in the manufacturing districts like Manchester. Unlike the public houses, the beerhouses were not supervised by the police. Consequently, the magistrates were virtually powerless to stop the rapid escalation in their numbers. In the ten years up to 1853, the number of beerhouses in Manchester rose up to 1572, an increase of 791, by contrast, the number of public houses actually decreased in the same period from 502 to 484.

Dr. Kay exclaimed, "the decency of our towns is violated, even in this respect, that every street blazons forth the invitations of these haunts of crime. Gin shops and beerhouses encouraged by law – Beer Act 1830 – and taverns, over which the police can at present exercise but an imperfect control, have multiplied with such rapidity that they will excite the strong remonstrances which every lover of good order is prepared to make with goverment, against the permission, much less the sanction of such public enormities." [6].

It must also be borne in mind that the pub had several socially beneficial features which must be granted due consideration alongside these sweeping denunciations. Often it provided the only means of escape from the dull toil and decadent surroundings for the working population. What's more it was the only place where groups, clubs and societies could meet in large numbers. In fact, many workmen were forced to meet in pubs to collect their wages which were often paid to one man in a large sum so that his workmates were induced to cash the note across the bar in order to divide it into smaller proportions. [7].

The criminal statistics contain comparatively few references to arrests for rioting, or politically motivated crimes. This would induate, at least in 1842, that Chartism in Manchester was not a very potent force.

Manchester's criminal class was like the wider society itself, hierarchically structured. At the top of the heap sat the swell mobsman, who could so easily be mistaken for a gentleman or 'Dandy'. "Except to their immediate associates," wrote a prison governor, "they appear and are considered gentlemen." They regularly loitered about the Exchange, the Banks and clearing-houses. They worked in teams. One of them, followed by a boy, would walk into a bank and take up a pen and begin to write. He would watch the movements of customers collecting money at the counters. In case he aroused anyone's suspicions he would have already armed himself beforehand with a cheque on another bank as a "stall-off" or a "blind." If he was stopped or questioned he could then plead ignorance to the wrong bank. He would wait to see into which pocket the money was put and then he and the boy would follow their victim into the street where the others were waiting. The boy would give the sign and two accomplices would bear down on the victim and with comparative ease effect their object, being assisted by the many facilities which the streets and lanes through which he passed afforded them.

Mobsmen often congregated together at their favourite haunts in the town, as observed by A.B. Reach in 1849, "There is a tavern here – Blakely Street, now called Charter Street – with a coloured lamp like that of a doctors, called the Dog and Duck. This is the house of call for the swell mob of Manchester and the superior class of prigs (thieves). [8]

The first class thieves would follow an entirely different pattern as they moved around the country, even visiting the continent on occasion. "They work the Dover packets, and visit The Lakes of Killarney. They go on the Manchester Exchange, and sleep in the hotels of New York. They know the way to the Liverpool Docks, and 'wine' in the Streets of Paris. They generally go on the Continent in the spring, and remain there until the races and fairs are coming off in England. The London mobs go down to Manchester in December, there being a large number of commercial men about the town at that time." [9]

Thieving was a specialised job; the stealing of a gentleman's handkerchief by a "buzzer," for instance required a different technique from thimble screwing (stealing a pocket watch). Shoplifting was regarded as a skilled and lucrative craft. Less prestigious were the sneakmen, theives who robbed tills in shops, stole goods from carts, or took goods from displays outside markets or shops. Then there were the horsestealers, embezzlers and forgers; and of course the important fences or receivers of stolen goods. A well known Manchester fence was "One-Armed Dick," who lived in a shop off Oldham Road, another was Joe Hyde landlord of the London Tavern.

Thieving had its customs and regulations like any other craft. A rough apprenticeship began at the age of 6 or 7, when as a ragged urchin the young thief tried his hand at petty pilfering. From stealing oranges off stalls he soon moved on to more difficult jobs, and with some advice and training from adult criminals, like "One-Armed Dick," he graduated to the ranks of the sneakmen, and, if he were lucky to the swell mobsmen.

TABLE SHOWING AGES OF THOSE APPREHENDED IN 1843

	MALES	FEMALES
Under 10 Years	30	16
Above 10 Years and Under 15 Years	445	80
Above 15 Years and Under 20 Years	1307	659
Above 20 Years and Under 25 Years	1754	968
Above 25 Years and Under 30 Years	1313	646
Above 35 Years and Under 40 Years	1972	748
Above 40 Years and Under 50 Years	1063	347
Above 50 Years and Under 60 Years	442	121
Above 60 Upwards	163	73

At the bottom of the heap were the vagrants. That vagrancy

JOSEPH NADIN
From a Print in the Chetham Library.

1   Joseph Naden, Deputy Constable of
     Manchester, 1802-20

2   Watchman

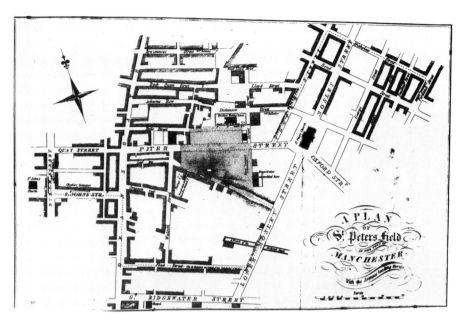

3a   Plan of St. Peters' Field,
Manchester. 1819

3b   Manchester Police on Parade, 1845

4   Sergeant Charles Brett, killed by
Fenians, 1867

5   Detective Jerome Caminada

6a   Police Horse Ambulance, circa 1895

6b   Pauper Children aided by Police
      Charity, 1901

7   William Henry Palin, Chief Constable,
     1858-1879

8   Charles Malcolm Wood, Chief
     Constable, 1879-1898

was the nursery of crime was accepted as axiomatic; habitual tramps became first beggars, then thieves and finally convicts. In early Victorian Manchester, like most large townships, beggars were sometimes ubiquitous, ingenious and colourful. The streets and thoroughfares contained a whole section of the population who lived by soliciting alms from passers-by. Some claimed to be ex-sailors and army veterans who had deserved well of their country. Others said they were distressed operatives, decayed gentlemen, shipwrecked mariners, blown-up miners, or burnt out salesmen. There were beggars who paraded their children, showed real or pretended sores, or exhibited themselves half-clad in cold weather in order to arouse pity. The blind, crippled, maimed and paralysed displayed themselves. There were 'artists' who chalked on the pavement, and sellers of matches and bootlaces. They were of all ages and of both sexes. Their object was to trade on the consciences of others more fortunate than themselves.

A major vagrancy problem for the police were the thousands of deserted, orphaned and runaway children found roaming the streets. Estimates of the number of these youngsters in Manchester were clear evidence that the problem was widespread and tragic. From May to the beginning of September, 1835, 471 children were reported lost and, over the same period only 138 were located and returned to their parents or the workhouse. For the years 1832-35 Manchester's police counted 8,650 deserted children in the town alone. [10].

Great numbers of children were brought before the courts for a plethora of vagrancy offences. One case involved a young girl named Ann Wild found wandering in the streets at a late hour and taken to the Central Police Office. Despite the fact that she lived in Back Piccadilly Street and her father was employed as a shoemaker, she had a long history of vagrancy, a fact which prompted the Magistrates to sentence her to hard labour for two months.

Contemporaries had no doubt that the criminal class was substantially a phenomenon of the large towns. J. T. Burt wrote in 1863, that the large towns were the nurseries and hiding places of criminal classes, and dense populations gave shelter to criminals. Manchester was fast becoming the most overcrowded town in the country. In 1834, the population had risen to 235,139, an increase of 48,000 when compared to the 1831 figure of 187,000.

The Reverend J. Clay, Chaplain of Preston Gaol, wrote in 1849, "it is not manufacturing Manchester, as such, which fosters crime. It is multitudinous Manchester which gives birth to whatever criminality may be imputable to it. It is the large town to which both idle and profligates and practised villains resort as a likely field for the indulgence of sensuality or the prosecution of schemes of plunder. It is the large town in which disorder and crime are generated."

Not only was Manchester's population increasing at a rapid rate but it was almost exclusively working-class. The smoke, stench and noise of industrialisation was fast driving the middle-classes out of the township and into the suburban districts of Hulme, Chorlton-upon-Medlock and Ardwick, whilst the swelling hordes of the labouring poor were crowded into the poorest districts of Ancoats, Deansgate and Angel Meadow where accommodation was cheapest.

This transformation was described by Frederick Engels in 1844. *"The town itself is peculiarly built, so that a person may live in it for years, and go out daily without coming into contact with a working people's quarter or even with workers, that is, so long as he confines himself to his business or to pleasure walks. This arises chiefly from the fact that by unconscious tacit agreement, as well as with outspoken conscious determination, the working people's quarters are sharply separated from the sections of the city reserved for middle class; or if this does not succeed, they are concealed with the cloak of charity. Manchester contains at its heart, a rather extended commercial district, perhaps half a mile long and about as broad and consisting almost wholly of offices and warehouses. Nearly the whole district is abandoned by dwellers and is lonely and deserted at night; only watchmen and policemen transverse its narrow lanes with their dark lanterns."* (11)

Just as the physical separation of the middle and working classes was taking place, so the political gulf between the two industrial classes was also widening. A manifestation of this separation was the Chartist movement.

In the spring of 1848, in a period of severe trade depression, Manchester's "peaceful period" was interrupted by a series of mass meetings and demonstrations attended by the impoverished handloom weavers, unemployed cotton mill operatives, and an assortment of artisans, who together made up the mass membership of the chartists.

Chartists were so named because they formulated their demands in a six point political charter: universal manhood suffrage, annual parliaments; vote by secret ballot, abolition of the property qualification of M.P.'s, payment of M.P.'s, and equal electoral districts. The object was to make the charter the law of the land, by legal, constitutional means if possible, or by force if necessary — or by a mixture of both. Politically Chartism was in the central tradition of British Radicalism stretching back to the corresponding societies of 1792, and Peterloo 1819, and the Chartists were proud of their heritage. It was a tradition of mass meetings, imprisonments and conflicts. Its membership in the Manchester district was composed mainly of a hardcore of handloom weavers and an assortment of artisans and cotton factory workers.

One of the heroes of Northern Chartists was the flamboyant Irish orator Feargus O'Connor who claimed to be the champion of the "unshorn chins, blistered hands and fustian jackets."

In March, rioting broke out in New Cross and mass meetings were organised to promote fraternisation between the Chartists and the Irish repealers who had a large following in that district.

It was estimated that there was 34,000 Irish people living in Manchester in 1841, Leon Faucher described their being in a perpetual state of agitation. "Often they assemble by hundreds at the corners of Oldham Road and at Ancoats. One of their number reads in a loud voice the Irish News, the addresses of O'Connell or the circulars of the Repeal Association; and afterwards the whole is commented upon without end and with great clamour. They are so strictly organised that in the twinkling of an eye, one or two thousand can be collected at any given spot." [12]

By April, there were strong fears of a planned Chartist insurrection and the authorities immediately reacted by swearing in 12,000 special constables.

On the 10th April (the day of the giant Chartist Demonstration at Kennington Common, London) Manchester was stripped for action — "cannon were found planted in the streets and dragoons patrolled the chief thoroughfare with drawn swords. Thousands of miners and factory hands marched out of Oldham, Ashton and other manufacturing townships, many of them with pikes and other implements of war." [13]

The setting was unpleasantly similar to Peterloo, and to the Newport rising of 1839, when thousands of Welsh miners were "checked by a fierce burst of musketry". But at Manchester in 1848, no attempt was made to take the marchers by surprise or to shoot them down; "as they approached the city they were warned of the danger that confronted them, and were persuaded to return to their homes." The new-fangled police methods of Willis and his contemporaries made for duller history, but less frequent bloodshed.

There followed a series of police raids in and around Manchester, as the authorities attempted to clamp down on the Chartist conspirators. Axon described the police activities in the Ancoats district. "At ten o'clock on the night of August 3rd, a force of three-hundred police constables was concentrated at the Oldham Road Station, and there formed into five divisions under the command of Captain Willis, Mr. Beswick and the different superintendents of the Manchester force. These bodies of policemen made a simultaneous visit to the chartist clubrooms in the neighbourhood of Ancoats and Oldham Road and arrested the following persons: James Leach, Thomas Whittaker, Henry Ellis, Daniel Donovan, John Finnigan, Patrick Devlin, Michael Corrigan, George Rogers, Thomas Rankin, Joshua Lemon, Henry Williams, George Webber, George White, Thomas Dowlin and Samuel Kearns." [14]

Actually Manchester weathered the Chartist storms more successfully than did some other Lancastrian townships, and this strengthened the Watch Committee's position when the Borough Council, in 1850, had to face strong ratepaying opposition calling for a reduction in the expense of the force. The Chief Constable cited the occurance of 1848 to strengthen his claim, "with regard to the total number of the police force, the present number (469) is rather the minimum required than otherwise, and hardly sufficient for the ordinary state of the borough. In times of excitement the importance of an efficient force cannot be overstated." [15]

The Chief Constable could also cite the remarkable improvement in the force's general efficiency since its inception. In 1846 for example, trade became exceedingly depressed and great privations were borne by the working-classes, in consequence not only of a shortage of work and a reduction in wages, but also the high price of necessaries. Yet during the same period "the Borough has been in a quiet a state, and freer from every description of crime than it's ever been known or shown to have been published," reported Captain Willis.

Apprehensions for the year totalled 7,629, the lowest figure so far recorded. Bearing in mind that the primary object of the police was the prevention of crime, these figures represent a successful year's work record.

One reason for the great reduction in apprehensions and criminality in general was the improving efficiency of the force through an awareness of its dependance upon public goodwill. The Chief Constable issued a series of instructions designed to widen the discretionary powers of the constables and avoid unnecessary apprehensions. One instruction laid down that in circumstances where an offence of a trivial nature has been committed then it is deemed expendient to take the offender's name and address and summon him before the Court instead of taking him into custody. In cases of disputes and quarrels between inhabitants, and when actual fighting has not been resorted to, or a breach of the peace committed, then it is better to attempt a reconciliation between the parties, than to resort to the exercise of their legal powers.

"By adopting this conciliatory course of action many unnecessary apprehensions were avoided, order has been re-established and maintained, and a better and more kindly feeling has been induced, without any compromise of duty between the inhabitants and the police force," reported Captain Willis.

The general conduct of the policemen themselves had also exhibited a marked improvement by 1846. This was aided by the establishment of a merit class of constables at an increased rate of wages, and the formation of a fund for the relief of those who might be injured in the service.

The new merit class consisted of 123 constables, from this number 14 were promoted to the rank of sub-inspector, 3 were recommended for positions in other forces, 5 were punished by a reduction in rank, and none were dismissed..

Of the class of ordinary constables consisting of 248 persons, 50 were promoted to the merit class, 2 were placed on the superannuated list and 22 were dismissed.

Of the sub-inspectors consisting of 45 persons, 5 were promoted to the rank of Inspector, one was reduced in rank and one dismissed.

The total number of dismissals during the year from the force of 469 persons was 24, whilst in the preceeding year it amounted to 48, and in the year 1844 to 99, and in both instances with a force of much small numbers.

Captain Willis reported, "As respects the conduct of the officers and constables and the working of the police establishment it affords me great pleasure to have it in my power to state that the returns exhibit a very marked improvement in the general behaviour of the force."

As proof of the propriety of the conduct of the police, it may be added that a total of £2,472 was taken from four thousand plus prisoners arrested for offences of drunkeness, and the whole amount restored to them when sober.

The Watch Committee not only supported the Chief Constable's contention that "if a police force is to be maintained at all, it ought to be made efficient," but went even further, "that so far as relates to the expense of the force, your committee may challenge comparison with the expenditure incurred in the maintenance of any other police force throughout the Kingdom." The committee was confident that when all the facts had been properly considered there would be no further talk of reducing the police force, but rather of strengthening it.

And strengthen the force they did. In 1848 the total manpower of the police force numbered 469, by 1858 this figure had increased to 604. It was becoming all too evident that the fortunes of the force were intricately linked to public approval, and if the ratepayers were willing to pay for increased protection, they got it.

NOTES - Chapter Six (Cont) - (1) J.J. Tobias, Crime and Industrial Society in the 19th century, p.106. (2) L. Faucher, Manchester 1844, p.41-42. (3) A.B. Reach, Manchester and the Textile Districts 1849, p.19. (4) B.P.P., S.C. on Public Houses 1853, Vol.37, Q.3714. (5) Ibid. Q.6104. (6) J. Kay, The Moral and Physical Condition of the Working Classes in Manchester. p.59. (7) B.P.P., S.C. on Drunkeness 1834 Q.594. (8) A.B. Reach, Manchester and the Textile Districts, 1849, p.54-56. (9) Cornhill Magazine, Vol.6, November 1862, p.650. (10) B.P.P. Accounts and Papers related to Deserted Children, 1836, Vol.41, p.23. (11) F. Engels, The Condition of the Working Class in England, p.79. (12) L. Faucher, Manchester 1844 p.28. (13) M. Hovell, History of the Chartist Movement, p.319. (14) W.E.A. Axon, Annals of Manchester, p.246. (15) Proceedings of the Borough Council, 27/3/1850.

Chapter Seven

CAPTAIN WILLIAM HENRY PALIN

A symbolic turning point in 19th century Manchester was Queen Victoria's visit in 1851, the year of the Great Exhibition. "The streets were immensely full," the Queen wrote in her diary, "and the cheering and enthusiasm most gratifying. The order and good behaviour of the people who were not placed behind the barriers, were the most complete we have seen in our many progressions through the capitals and cities, for there never was a running crowd. Nobody moved, and therefore everybody saw well and there was no squeezing. Everyone says that in no other town could one depend so entirely upon the quiet and orderly behaviour of the people as in Manchester. You had only to tell them what ought to be done and it was sure to be carried out."

Queen Victoria had correctly perceived a mood of optimsm and well being among Manchester's working-class population. The economy was showing a marked improvement, the empire was growing and with it the markets for our manufactured goods. In consequence, employment increased and wage levels started to rise. The old antagonisms which had been collectively channelled into Chartism, were gradually being eroded. Manchester's working men, at least the more respectable elements, were now more likely to be found subscribing to Samuel Smile's ethic of Self-Help and to the modern idea of Cooperative Societies, rather than any notion of revolution or alternative societies. Clearly, a new optimistic age was dawning.

In 1857, after fifteen years as Manchester's Chief Constable, Captain Willis retired from the force to take up a newly created post as a Government Inspector of Constabulary. He was the third Inspector to be appointed, the first was Lt. Col. John Woodford, the former Chief Constable of Lancashire, with whom Willis served prior to his appointment at Manchester. The second was Major General Cartwright, a veteran of the Peninsular

War and Waterloo, who seems to have had no previous police experience. The Home Secretary admonished them "to secure the goodwill and the cooperation of the local authorities, and expressed his reliance on their "judgement, temper and discretion." Their immediate task was to appraise the state of the efficiency of two hundred and thirty seven separate forces in England and Wales, and to pay the limited Exchequer grant to those certified as efficient in point of numbers and discipline.

Lt. Col. Woodford took charge of the Northern District, Cartwright the Midlands and Willis the Southern District. Manchester formed part of the district under Mr. Woodford's jurisdiction. In his first inspection report, Mr. Woodford remarked that the Manchester force consisted of five hundred and twenty two officers and constables and "was composed of a remarkably fine and effective body of men, most of them in the prime of life and health."

One of the tests of "efficiency" applied by the Inspectors was the ratio of police to population. The County Police Act of 1839* imposed a maximum of one constable per thousand of population, a figure well in excess of Manchester's ratio of one constable per five hundred and forty of population. Not many of the police forces in the Northern district were reported on quite so favourably as Manchester. Often the station-houses and lock-ups which were taken over from the parish authorities were severely criticised by Woodford. Some in Northumberland were found to be so isolated and accessible from all sides that, it was reported, "prisoners had been put in sober and taken out drunk"; and in some of the small boroughs "no police office is established or books kept." At Rochdale, the local officials sent a protest to the Home Secretary about three of their policemen – Fowler, Leary and Twist – who had abused and threatened Alice Roberts in the "Three Crowns Inn," one of them going so far as to "thrust his head up her petticoats."

Wigan provides an amusing illustration of most of the features in a smaller establishment. A Manchester policeman called Thomas advised the local Watch Committee to have a

* Manchester being a town with more than 10,000 inhabitants, was exempt from the terms of the Act, but non-the-less the figure served, as a useful guide.

body of preventative police forty strong, but the Committee plumped for six only. Thirty five applied for the six posts, of whom the only one with experience appointed was John Whittle, and he was appointed Chief Constable. A Superintendent of the Manchester Watch, a Deputy Constable of Pendleton, a Sheriff's Officer of Derby, a man with eighteen years experience with the Glasgow Police, and another with eight years with the Liverpool police were ignored. All of those appointed were from Wigan, the first being a man called Hugh Fegan, who had a relative Richard Fegan, sitting on the Watch Committee.

The records show that Hugh Fegan was "admonished" by the Mayor because his prisoners tended to become "more intoxicated than when put into prison." Eventually Fegan was dismissed for making false entries in the books.

The pay and conditions of Manchester's constables compared favourably with those of other forces in the Northern Division. For "ordinary" constables the pay ranged from 25s. 1d. to 21s. 6d. per week; probationary constables started at 19s. 8d. and gradually, over the first two years, they advanced to the lower rate of an "ordinary" constable. Out of the 52 forces which constituted the Northern Division, only three paid their constables a higher wage and only two paid the same.

Manchester's constables also contributed 5d. per week to the force's superannuation fund. If, after 15 years service, a constable was forced to retire because of disablement he could reckon upon a pension of at least one third his salary, and upon a higher rate upon retirement after completing 20 years service. Retirement pensions for policemen were not universal, for example, at neighbouring Ashton-under-Lyne, there was no retiring pension after even longer service. [1].

As might be expected, the constables were not always indifferent to the salaries which were imposed upon them. In 1853, two hundred and fifty constables in Manchester gave a month's notice of resignation over a demand for higher wages and were only persuaded to withdraw their appeal on the assurance of the Superintendents that a more moderate request would be greeted with greater favour.

So far as it can be said that national policies for the police began to emerge, these policies were now for the first time being formulated by the Government Inspectors in the light of what they discovered; and their conclusions, duly reported annually to the Home Secretary, at last placed the Home Office in a position to adopt its own policies – if it cared to do so. But policy making in the Whitehall of the mid 19th century was in its infancy.

Captain Willis's successor was another ex-Army Captain, Captain William Henry Palin. Born in India, Captain Palin was educated in England up to being sixteen when he enlisted in the 17th Bombay Native Infantry. He subsequently became adjutant, paymaster, quartermaster and interpreter. In 1856 he resigned his captaincy and returned to England.

During the early years of Palin's period in office a policy of economic stringency resulted in a favourable surplus of receipts over expenditure, which in 1866 amounted to £2,597 10s. 8d.

The entire annual cost was £65,000 0s. 0d. made up as follows:-

The commissioner (Colonel Fraser) received a salary of £1000; the chief superintendent £600; the police surgeon £500; the receiver £350; the superintendent received a weekly wage of £4. 18s. 6d; two Inspectors received £3. 6s. 7d., and twelve Inspectors received wages ranging from £2.11s. 3d. to £3.1s.6d., fourteen station sergeants and fourteen detective sergeants received each £2. 1s. 0d; twenty eight sergeants £1.14s. 10d; and twenty eight "2nd class" sergeants £1. 11s. 9d. per week; 296 constables received £1. 8s. 8d; 165 constables £1. 5s.1d; and 129 constables £1. 1s. 6d.

There was an allowance paid to 48 plain clothes constables of 5s. per week each, and to one Inspector, twelve sergeants and forty eight constables, in lieu of uniform £376. 2s. 8d. Every officer and Constable received 3s. 0d. per month as boot money. The total payment in salaries and allowances was £52,345. 0s. 4d.

Clothing, helmets, stocks and armlets cost for the year £2,951 0s. 2d; lanterns and oil £310; necessaries for infirmary £400; rates, rents and taxes £2,993; coals and gas £895; furniture and bedding £50; repairs to police stations £300; printing and stationary £300; and disbursements and miscellaneous payments £1,012. Evidently, the "top hats" worn by the first policemen were being replaced by helmets in 1866.

The estimated income for the ensuing year was £67,161 9s.2d;

and was derived from the following sources:-

Produce of 8d. in the £ on the assessable rental of the city — £1,518,332 — after deducting 6% for poundage and deficiencies, £47,575; proportion of expenses from city's cash £15,17516s.6d; estimated fines and penalties £550; payment out of Bridge-House Estate for watching London and Blackfriars Bridges £668 4s. 0d; payment for men on private service at the Bank, the Post-Office, Blackwall Railway, City of London Union, Inland Revenue Office, Times Office, Guildhall Justice-Room, Messrs. Gooch and Cousens, Messrs. Parson and Co., Messrs. Kearns, Major and Field, and as assistant gaolers and omnibus time-keepers, £2114 4s. 8d. [2].

Such favourable accounts may well have pleased the rate-payers of Manchester, but not all of Manchester's citizens were satisfied with the protection afforded them by their local guardians. Local newspapers of the period published a steady stream of letters each complaining about alleged nuisances and general lawlessness. On the 18th October, 1865, the following letter appeared in the Manchester Courier:

"May I request you through the medium of your valuable paper to give publicity to the disgraceful scenes which are daily occuring in Deansgate, and which requires immediate legal prevention. Yesterday week, as I was returning from St. John's church after divine service with my wife and daughter, I saw two women half-naked and in a state of beastly drunkenness, fighting with a man in Deansgate. I walked some distance past there with my wife and daughter, requested them to walk home, and then returned. On my return the crowd dispersed for it is but justice to say that the utmost respect is generally paid to a clergy-man. I waited, however, until a policeman (No. 105) came up, who told me it was impossible for him to prevent such scenes. On the Monday I called to see Captain Palin, who, after an hours waiting, told me he would do his best to ensure order.

Yesterday however, as I was returning in a cab to St. John's to perform a funeral service, I saw two men with their coats off fighting in Deansgate. Having no time to wait, I requested the driver to go on, which he did with some difficulty, through a crowd of fifty to one hundred persons, who were looking-on shouting, and many of them encouraging the combattants. Today I called again on Captain Palin who said to me that it was impossible for him, with the force at his disposal, to maintain law and order. It becomes therefore, a question whether mob rule or the law of the land is to prevail in Manchester."

Yours etc. W. M. HUNTINGTON,
RECTOR OF ST. JOHN'S CHURCH.

Four days later a second letter appeared:

"Sir, the public generally are much indebted to Mr. Huntington for calling their attention to the state and discipline of the police force, more especially at the present period, with winter approaching, when the efficiency of such a force is of vital importance to us all. Mr. Huntington's letter has also been the means of eliciting the important fact, which I should otherwise have doubted that there is actually a Superintendent of police in or near Manchester. From the illdisciplined and irregular way in which the police walk, or rather stray about the streets, I should have supposed that they had no commander, but were merely left to follow their own will and pleasure. Instead of policemen pacing the streets separately as in other towns, you seldom meet a policeman who is not accompanied by another, and at many of the corners of the streets you may observe three of them gossiping together. No doubt it is more agreeable to policemen, like other people to walk in pairs than to wander alone; but we do not pay police to do what is most pleasant to themselves, but to protect our persons and our property from such outrages as those of which Mr. Huntington complains. It is obvious that if the police were properly dispersed about, half the present force would be as efficient as the entire force now is."

SIGNED – A RATEPAYER.

The following story appeared in the same paper headed, 'Boy stoned by Policemen'.*"A scandalous scene was enacted in Canal Street yesterday, about one o'clock. A lad was bathing in the canal, and police sergeant 9c and constable 85c commenced pelting him with stones as a means of compelling him to come out of the water. This sport was continued for some time. An immense crowd assembled from the adjoining streets, and great indignation was expressed at the conduct of the police, which appeared to terrify the lad, who showed no inclination to trust himself in the hands of the assailants. At last a man got hold of the boy, and dragged him out on the other side. A third policeman, who had come up took hold of the boy's clothes and attempted to throw them across the canal; but in so doing they fell into the water and became soaked with wet. It was discovered that the lad was severly cut and bruised about the back of his body by the stones which had been hurled at him; and two of the wounds were said to be large enough to lay a finger in. The constables sought to force the boy to dress himself in his wet clothes so that after his stoning he might be marched off in triumph to dry himself within the chill precincts of a police-cell; but a Mr. Kay and two gentlemen who had witnessed the disgraceful occurrance remonstrated with the officers in a determined manner. Meantime the street had become alive with people, and was literally "in arms". The lad was taken in to a shed, where he had a fit. The police were mobbed and hooted at in the most vigorous fashion; and were in turn treated to a taste of stoning, which speedily made them take to flight, amidst groans, laughter and yells, both loud and deep. The lad was wrapped up in a shirt and conveyed to the Royal Infirmary."* [3].

Evidently, the force's public image had become tarnished and this prompted fears that Manchester was becoming a most decadent city.

Captain Palin inserted a curt reply to the Reverend Huntington, which appeared in a later edition of the Courier. "Unfortunately, the police have abundant occupation in that district — Deansgate — and to prove that they are not inattentive to their duties it is only necessary to say that on reference to the books I find between the 1st September and the 18th October last, no fewer than 411 persons were taken into custody in Deansgate and neighbourhood."

A comparison between criminality in Manchester and other towns of relative size is a study in itself, however certain differences appear from even the most cursory examination. The link between Manchester and Liverpool is an obvious one, not only because both towns enjoyed similar rates of growth and were geographically close together, but each town was influenced by the criminal activity in the other. What one finds most striking about Liverpool is the amount of crime committed there. In a report by the Reverend Clay, Chaplain of Preston Gaol, he claimed that in Liverpool there were twice as many arrested in 1848 as in Manchester, Salford, Bolton and Preston put together. Also the number of females arrested in Liverpool was three times greater than in the other four towns; summary convictions were three and a half times greater, and convictions for robberies were more than seventeen times greater than the other four towns. [4].

Some of the reasons for the high criminality in Liverpool are clear from the nature of the two towns. Liverpool was a seaport and thus harboured thousands of sailors, crewmen, travellers and other foreigners who, no doubt, served as a disorderly influence within the town. Liverpool was also the principal port of call for the many Irish who spilled over to England in their thousands after the potato crises in 1846. Father Nugent, Chaplain at Liverpool Gaol had reported that the Irish were more criminal in England since poverty in Ireland did not afford the same market facilities for crime. [5].

Whether Manchester was more criminal than other large towns is not so important as the fact that it was regarded as such by thieves and vagabonds all over England. "If you say in any other part of England that you are from Manchester, you are at once supposed to be a thief; it is the same with London, Birmingham and Liverpool; but they say that Manchester and Birmingham turn out more thieves than London and Liverpool." [6].

NOTES - (1) Manchester Examiner and Times, 9/12/1867. (2) Ibid. 27/11/1866. (3) Manchester Courier, 14/7/1866. (4) "26th Report of the Preston House of Correction", Lanc's County Gaols Chaplain's Reports, 1849, p.15. (5) B.P.P., S.C. on Prisons 1870, Vol.8, p.51. (6) Juvenile Delinquency in Manchester, W.B.Neale, p.58.

Chapter Eight

MURDER OF SERGEANT BRETT

The Fenian Movement, which had taken up arms against British rule in Ireland, was spreading its activities to metropolitan Britain. The Irish Republican Brotherhood, as the movement was known in Ireland, was stiffened by many officers who had served with distinction in the American Civil War. Two of them, Colonel Kelly and Captain Deasy were among those who eluded the police and crossed the Irish Sea to reorganise and raise the morale of the Fenian groups in England. Both Irish Americans, their accents alone were bound to arouse suspicion, but curiously they were arrested after being seen loitering in the early hours of 11th September, in Oak Street, Shudehill. Two of their colleagues managed to escape and at that time the police, unaware of the identity of their captives, merely suspected them of plotting to rob a shop. They were charged under a Vagrancy Act and remanded in custody. Meanwhile communications with the Irish Authorities revealed their true identity.

After their identification, Kelly and Deasy were remanded by the Magistrates with a view to their being transferred to the city gaol at Belle Vue, Hyde Road. Telegrams from Dublin and the Home Office warned the police of a possible attempt to release them.

Once the proceedings were concluded a horse drawn prison van was drawn up outside the front of the police court, Police Constables Shaw and Yarwood, with Detectives Bromley and Taylor, were positioned on the box; Constables Knox and Connell were seated behind. Inside the van was the illfated Sergeant Brett, known to all as "Charlie".

The van was in effect a portable prison, divided into two rows of cells by a corridor and only very dimly lit through overhead ventilators and the grating on the door. The seven guards carried no arms and were equipped only with staves, while the keys to the van were carried inside by Sergeant Brett who alone could give access to the prisoners or allow their release.

A number of prisoners were being transported in the van, but Kelly and Deasy were kept handcuffed in separate compartments, unable to communicate with one another. Behind the van there followed a cab containing more policemen. Their additional presence was obviously dictated by the importance of their charges Kelly and Deasy, not by the occupants of the other cells which housed three prostitutes and a boy being taken to the reformatory.

An account of what followed on that afternoon of Wednesday 18th September, 1867, is vividly described by the reporter from The Times:

"This morning the supposed Colonel Kelly and Captain Deasy, having been remanded by the Magistrates were placed in a cell with a view to removal to the city gaol, Belle Vue. About 3 o'clock the van was drawn up in front of the police court to remove all the prisoners to gaol and among them the two Fenians. At this time the police noticed two men hanging about whom they suspected to be Fenians, and a policeman made a rush at one of them to arrest him, in which he succeeded, but not till the man had drawn a dagger and attempted to stab him. The blow was avoided. The other suspected person made his escape. In consequence of this Kelly and Deasy were put in irons before being taken to the van. When the van left the city it had to proceed over Ardwick Green and along Hyde Road, a fine open street leading to the gaol, and nearly a mile in length; it was drawn by two horses and was guarded behind by seven policemen. The van had proceeded about half a mile up the road when on passing under the viaduct which carries the London and North Western Railway across, with an open field on the right, a volley of shots were fired at it. The policemen not seeing where the shots came from, dropped off the van and spread themselves out wide. There was a rush of 30 to 40 Irishmen upon the police and upon the van. One man had a hatchet, another a hammer, and a third a bayonet with which they set to work to break open the van. One man took a revolver and

fired into the lock. Ultimately men with large stones broke through the top of the van and the panels of the door behind, and set all the prisoners, including the two Fenians, at liberty. The policemen collected in a body and made a rush to prevent the prisoners being liberated but several revolvers were discharged among them, and one constable was shot over one of his eyes, and was taken to the infirmary. A young man, a bystander, was shot through the head. It is expected the Fenians, being in irons, will be recaptured. The streets of Manchester have been in a state of great excitement all the evening. The officer shot in the head is named as Sergeant Brett. The ball passed through his head and lodged in his hat. William O'Meara Allen, said to have fired the fatal shot, was chased and taken. Detective Bromley received a shot in one of his thighs. Another policeman was shot in his back. Both the horses were shot. The driver of the van was knocked off his box with a stone. A dozen arrests have been made. The two Fenians are still at liberty but a squadron of Dragoons are passing the Telegraph Office, guarding a carriage, at this moment, which may contain further important captives. "[1]

The Times story was inaccurate in at least one detail. Kelly and Deasy were not recaptured in spite of their being in "irons". At first the police suspected they were hidden in Ancoats, a strong Fenian district, and numerous raids were made on houses occupied by the Irish population. Within three days more than 50 suspects were in custody.

Finally, twenty six men were charged with an assortment of major crimes, headed with the capital offence of Murder. One of the principle prosecution witnesses was Constable George Shaw. He identified William O'Meara Allen, Michael Larkin, William Gould (a pseudonym for O'Brien), Edward Shore (whose real name was later established as Condon) and Thomas Maguire, as taking part in the events beneath the Railway Arches in Hyde Road. But, to be fair to him, he expressed some doubt about Maguire saying that he thought he was there helping to break the van but that he did not get a clear look at him. (It was later discovered that Maguire was not implicated in the crime at all but was in fact a Marine on home leave and who happened to be passing the scene of the rescue at the relevant time).

Constable Shaw was positive in his identification of Allen as the man who fired the shot at Sergeant Brett. He testified to seeing Larkin and Shore (Condon) throwing stones, but could not swear to seeing revolvers in the hands of Gould and Shore (that is O'Brien and Condon).

Out of those charged, twelve were convicted. The five for murder and seven for riot and assault. The seven were: William Murphy, Brennan, Charles Moorhouse, John Carroll, Featherstone, Skelly and Reddin.

Immediately after the verdict was received a petition was drawn up to secure the release of Maguire. The petition, which was organised by leading members of the trial press, was addressed to the Home Secretary, who after careful study of the evidence announced that he had been given a "free pardon."

The petitioning did not end there. Three days before the date fixed for the executions — 25th November — The Times announced that "Her Majesty has been graciously pleased to respite the capital sentence upon the convict Shore, in whose favour it may be remembered that he was unarmed when apprehended and that he was not proved to have been armed during the fatal affray." The fact that Shore (Condon) was an American citizen no doubt played no small part in obtaining his reprieve. He went on to serve eleven years imprisonment before being deported to America.

At 8.00 a.m. on the morning of November 25th 1867 Allen, Larkin and O'Brien were hanged outside the walls of the New Bailey Gaol.

Security precautions were extensive. The authorities, acting on the instructions from the Home Office, had taken possession of New Bailey Street the day before, and under the command of Captain Sylvester,* it was policed by 500 men drawn from the Manchester, Salford and County Forces. The Manchester side of the river, Stanley Street, Albert Bridge and a short distance along New Bailey Street, was occupied by the Manchester police force under Captain Palin. Five hundred soldiers in and around the prison were augmented by two thousand ordinary and special constables occupying the surrounds of the prison and the area between the spectators.

* Chief Constable of Salford

A memorial to Sergeant Brett's bravery was "erected by members of the Manchester Police Force and Friends" at St. Barnabas's Church in Rodney Street off Oldham Road, where the sergeant had been a Churchwarden for many years. In 1959, the memorial stone was transferred to St. Anne's Church after St. Barnabas's was demolished.

A memorial to the three hanged men the "Manchester Martyrs" was erected in St. Joseph's Cemetary, Moston, in 1897.

In the aftermath of the escape, the reputation of the Manchester force did not rate so highly as did the acts of bravery of its individual officers. "I have never been so annoyed," wrote the Home Secretary, Mr. Hardy, after receiving news of Kelly's rescue.

It would appear that the extra precautions taken by the police were sadly inadequate in the light of the information placed before them by the Irish Authorities.

On the day of the escape a telegram was sent by the Chief Secretary to the Dublin Government, Lord Mayo, addressed to Superintendent Maybury of the Manchester Police. It read, "Are the prisoners lodged in Gaol? have every precaution taken for their safe custody. Let extra guards be provided, if necessary. Consult Williamson, (a Fenian expert based in England) telegraph reply."

The facts were that the telegram was sent from Dublin at 1.30 p.m. English time, arrived in Manchester at 1.55 p.m. and was delivered at 2.5 p.m. The prison van left the court for the gail at 3.30 p.m. In the absence of Superintendent Maybury, a junior clerk opened the telegram and handed it to an Inspector when he came on duty at 2.15 p.m. The Inspector went in search of another superintendent to whom he gave the contents of the telegram. The superintendent directed that seven or eight constables were to accompany the prison van, and that four others were to follow close behind. All the officers were unarmed.[2]

Home Secretary Hardy sent the following message to Mayo in Dublin: "The news that Kelly was captured arrived here – Balmoral by post at 6.0 o'clock and I was going to tell the Queen at dinner as she is greatly interested in all such matters when, while I was waiting for her to come down, a telegram came with the intelligence of the rescue. What has happened will awaken Englishmen to some notion of the incendiaries around them and make them take more interest in what so deeply affects Ireland. I agree with you that the police have been supine and if the information which has reached me tonight that Deasy has got to France be correct, negligence as well as apathy must be imputed to them."[3]

NOTES - (1) The Times, 19/9/1867.   (2) Leon O'Broin, Fenian Fever, p.195.
(3) Ibid. p.187.

Chapter Nine

MANCHESTER'S TOP DETECTIVE

Whatever the verdict on the Fenian tragedy, the Chief Constable was able to report in 1870 that the morale and general efficiency of the force had not been retarded.

In that year the force's establishment was 737, at which figure it had stood for the previous three years. Recruitment had more than compensated for the depletions brought about by resignations and retirements. That the morale would seem to be improving may be deduced from the fact that ten years earlier dismissals numbered 41, whereas in 1870-1 only 7 men were dismissed.

The average length of service was six years and 9 months, the vast majority of the men were young and inexperienced. Two hundred and thirty three men had joined during the previous two years; three hundred had been in the force under ten years; ninety nine from ten to fifteen years; fifty eight from fifteen to twenty years, and forty seven, twenty years upwards.

The strength of the force more than kept pace with the rising population of the borough during the period 1843-1870. In 1843 the size of the force was 398 and the population was 235,139, a ratio of 590.8 persons per policeman. In 1870, the 737 men of the police force were attendant upon 374,993 inhabitants, a ratio of 508.8 persons per policeman.

Each officer's workload increased quite alarmingly during this period. In 1860, the total number of persons proceeded against for both summary and indictable offences was 10,194. By 1870, the number had almost trebled to 26,084. What is more, the preventative quality of police-work was also showing an improved and encouraging trend. The criminal returns for the year showed a slight diminution in the number of crimes reported to the police of nearly 1,000. In 1870, 1365 persons were apprehended for 5,744 indictable offences, whereas in 1869 the figures were 1,369 persons apprehended and 6,794 indictable offences.

When account is taken of the social conditions endured by Manchester's labouring poor, it is amazing that so few crimes were actually committed. For example, in 1870 Manchester's 374,993 inhabitants were crowded into an area so small that the official density figure of 83.6 per acre was second only to Liverpool's in the national table. By comparison, Salford's figure was 23.5, London's 41.2 and Birmingham's 47.2 per acre.

In a survey conducted by the Manchester Guardian regarding the proliferation of slum dwellings and common lodging-houses in the city, the reporter returned to the districts described by Reach a quarter of a century before only to find that little had changed. Describing a common lodging house in Charter Street, Angel Meadow, he wrote,

"We enter out of a bright frosty air direct into the common room, a room which looks as it had once been a shop. It is dark and cold outside – inside it is ruddy with a glowing fire, and reeking with the damp of drying clothes and perspiring humanity. Eighteen adults and several babies of both sexes are here, seated on backless benches in a room about 14 ft. square. In one corner is an itinerant tinman and his wife busy soldering up pastry cutters. It is about 11 o'clock at night, and little Maggie their seven years old daughter who ought to have been in bed long ago, is busy watching and fetching the soldering irons. There, half asleep, propped up by the wall, sits a woman knitting cheap mats for ornaments; and in front of the fire is a vagrant blind singer who says he gets his living in the streets by "singing a few patriotic songs in the 'ould Irish style". One woman is brewing tea in a basin, and stirring it with a knife to give it a flavour. As for the rest, they are "cadgers" of all sorts and conditions; Listless, moody, almost sullen, they certainly do not talk, and scarcely seem to think, and their chief object appears to be to postpone as long as possible the terrible ordeal of going to bed. Nor do we wonder at this when we have seen what bed is like.

Of the bedrooms there are four, and in these four there are ten beds, each bed to hold two persons. The attic ceiling is black with damp and mould, and the wet drops through on to one of the beds. There is neither gas nor fire

here, and the cold damp chill which strikes us as we enter, explains the desire evinced by the occupants to take as much heat up to bed with them as possible. What the effect of this change must be is told by the racking cough of some of the huddled-up inmates who have already retired.

As for the moral effect, what can be expected where the beds are placed as close to each other as they well can be? There is no screen, no curtain, no provision for the common necessities of life — not even any appliances for washing; and "they washes when they wants to in a bowl on one of the forms in the kitchen," is the information we obtain in answer to what is evidently deemed an impertinent question."[1]

The same reporter then takes the reader into the Deansgate district.

"How prolific of vice the Deansgate quarter is, a few facts and figures will painfully demonstrate. Deansgate and its vicinity may be considered as the slum of the 'A' Division of the police. Our Guest leads us down divers courts, finding misery and infamy everywhere, places so bad that for charity's sake they ought to be suppressed. Here in Sotheran Court, up a narrow passage, through some half-fallen buildings, a small yard is reached, and in it are two houses that only hold themselves up from force of habit. According to all known laws they ought to fall, but they don't; they harbour a nest of women of the vilest kind who nightly take home with them the lowest and worst of thieves. The noises and debauchery carried on here are indescribable, and the neighbours dare not say anything for fear of the rowdyism which congregates there.

But the most startling feature of Deansgate is the enormous number of its ginshops, its public-houses, and its singing saloons. Even now, after last year's raid upon them, there is a great number left, and our research into the causes of crime and disease leads us to look into these places as originating sources of a good deal of both."[2]

The same conclusion was reached by one of Captain Palin's senior Detectives, Chief Inspector Jerome Caminada. He wrote, *"Such places as the 'Dog and Rat' the 'Red, White and Blue', the 'Old Ship,' the 'Pat M'Carthy,' the 'Green Man' and other equally notorious places were then in full swing as licensed beerhouses. Passing these, the pedestrian's ear would be arrested by the sound of music proceeding from the mechanical organs, accompanied sometimes with drums and tambourines . . . some rude attempt would be made at an indecent song by a half-drunken girl for the edification of some collier lads who were the chief victims of these haunts, but her voice would be drowned by the incessant quarrelling and obscene language of her companions.*"[3]

The same writer made the following perceptive observation, *"Drink, no doubt, is responsible for many of these people making their appearance in gaol; but surrounded as they are by a vast desert of bricks and mortar with nothing except the public house in their midst to enliven them, or to arouse pleasant emotions, is it to be wondered that women become drunken and intidy, and that men desert their homes for the public house, become selfish and brutal towards their families or that they and their children recruit the criminal classes? Wherever the ruling classes neglect their duties towards those over whom they are placed, they must take the consequences. If the rich man's horses and dogs are better housed, trained, and cared for than the children of the poor, then the dogs and horses will be more tractable and docile than the children.*"[4]

What happened to the children of the poor when, for the first time, they appeared before the Magistrates was described by Caminada,

"A boy was charged with stealing postage stamps and money from the drawer of the till in the cashier's office of the place where he was employed. After being detected, he was sentenced by the Stipendiary Magistrate to receive twelve strokes of the birch rod.

Before a juvenile is birched, the Police Surgeon – Dr. W. J. Heslop – examines him; he is then strapped to the horse, his wrists and ankles are strapped, and a body-belt goes over his back. These preliminaries are worse than the birching. The little fellow, not knowing what will really

*take place, shouts and screams during the strapping
process, making it painful to be within hearing. The
birching itself is not severe, but the effect is very deterrent,
and has prevented many juveniles from having to be sent
to prison. The police surgeon and a police Inspector have
to be present in every case of birching.* "[5] (During the
period of Caminada's service the court inspector responsible for
administering the birch was named Mason, "a stout, well-built
man with a large moustache.")

During his twenty eight years in the Manchester Detective
Department, Jerome Caminada became known as the most
outstanding detective in the force. Judge Parry of the
Manchester County Court described him as "the Garibaldi of
Detectives."

He was born in Manchester in 1844 of an Italian father and
spent some time as an engineering apprentice at Mather and
Platts ironworks before joining the police in 1868.

As a uniformed constable Caminada patrolled the city's
streets for three years before moving into the Detective
Department where he made his reputation as a fearless
investigator.

During his service in the Detective Department, Caminada
became the recipient of a great number of monetary gifts and
rewards from grateful robbery victims following his recovery of
their property. The Watch Committee also rewarded him with
gifts for his devoted service to the city including a special
pension of £210 per annum when he retired in 1899 as
Superintendent of Detectives.

It was not unusual for Caminada to receive a gift of £100
from a National Bank following a successful investigation of a
case of forgery or fraud. In one celebrated case a dispute arose
as to who was entitled to the reward offered for the arrest of a
man named Arthur Foster who had obtained £5,200 by forgery.
The dispute, involving Caminada and a man named Pingstone,
was heard at the local County Court and finally settled in
Pingstone's favour. Subsequently, a group of local gentlemen
sympathising with Manchester's famous detective raised a
subscription and presented him with three hundred guineas for
his good work in the case.[6]

Caminada died in 1914 at the age of seventy at his home

"Mount St. Bernard' Denmark Road, Moss Side. His obituary appeared in the Daily Dispatch, written by Judge Parry. "Manchester has lost a great character and a good citizen in Jerome Caminada, with his sterling value as a man and a detective. In the latter class he stood alone – he was a genius."

One of the most notorious of criminals in this era, and one who successfully evaded Caminada's giant shadow, was Charlie Peace.

Born Charles Frederick Peace on the 14th February, 1832, he was described as a "small, ugly, lame individual, taken to be as much as twenty years older than in fact he was."

A burglar by profession, Charlie Peace dressed very smartly and moved around the country in a confident and open manner claiming that in his experience the police did not suspect men who conducted themselves as gentlemen. In his pocket, he always carried a pistol.

He was 47 years old when, on the 25th February 1879, he was executed at Armley Prison for murdering Arthur Dyson, whose wife Charlie Peace hoped would soon become his mistress. During his brief stay in the condemned cell Charlie Peace confessed to murdering a Manchester Policeman in August, 1876, following his unsuccessful attempt to break into a house in Chorlton cum-Hardy. Peace's revelation was all the more dramatic since one, William Habron had already been convicted of the murder and sentenced to hang. Fortunately, the death sentence had been committed to life imprisonment by order of the Home Secretary.

The Manchester murder took place on the night of August 1st 1876. Police Constable 1015 Nicholas Cock paraded for duty that night at the Chorlton-cum-Hardy police station and was assigned to a beat covering the Brookes Bar district. He was just twenty years of age and had been a member of the Lancashire Constabulary for eight months. It was on a triangular piece of ground from which three main roads diverged, the Chorlton-cum-Hardy Road, Upper Chorlton Road, and Seymour Grove, that Constable Cock was shot dead.

The police mounted a thorough search of the neighbourhood. In a hut not far from the scene were found three brothers, William, Frank and John Habron, who were all known to the police. Constable Cock himself had only recently arrested them for disorderly behaviour. The brothers denied they had anything to do with the murder and explained that they were "sleeping-rough" in the hut because they hadn't any money for lodgings.

Police evidence was almost wholly circumstantial. Several witnesses testified that the brothers had vowed to avenge their arrests by an attack on Constable Cock. In addition, William Habron was identified as having spent some considerable time in a local shop pricing gun cartridges.

The case against Frank Habron was dismissed by local Magistrates because of insufficient evidence, but William and John Habron were sent to the Assize Court to be tried before Mr. Justice Lindley.

Charlie Peace was present throughout the two day hearing and won the admiration of his neighbours in the public gallery for his "expert knowledge of the law". The trial greatly interested me", he commented later, "I always had a liking to be present at trials".

The jury considered their verdict for two and a half hours before returning to find William "guilty" and John "not guilty". Donning his black cap, Mr. Justice Lindley passed the death sentence on 18 years old William. "I am innocent", he shouted as the warders led him away to his cell.

Charlie Peace's confession was accepted as genuine by the Home Office after a thorough enquiry into the case by Lancashire's Chief Constable. His report concluded that there was no reason to doubt Peace's truthfulness when facing the death sentence.

During the 1870's, Manchester's police force was split into five major divisions. The 'A' division, with its headquarters at Knott Mill Police Station, Deansgate, had 212 men under the command of Superintendent John Gee. The 'B' division, with its headquarters at Goulden Street, Collyhurst, had 159 men under the command of Superintendent Charles William Godby. The 'C' division with its headquarters at Fairfield Street, where 153 men were stationed under the command of Superintendent Thomas Anderton. The 'D' Division with its headquarters at Cavendish Street, had 164 men under the command of Superintendent Thomas Meade. And the 'E' division which was based at the force headquarters and was composed of the members of the Detective Department and Court Officers, together totalling 50 officers commanded by Superintendent Robert Coy.

The headquarters of the force were housed in the Town Hall building in King Street, up to 1877, when the present Town Hall building in Albert Square was formally opened by the then Mayor, Alderman Abel Heywood. The Chief Constable's offices were subsequently transferred across the city to take up part of the ground floor of the new building. The basement housed a police charge office and prison cells with admittance being gained from the Lloyd Street entrance.

In the same year as the new Town Hall was opened, a new and quite substantial police station was under construction in Willert Street, Collyhurst, later to become the Divisional Headquarters Building for the 'B' division. The necessity for a new station in the Collyhurst district was largely as a result of repeated attacks on policemen as they walked through the streets of Collyhurst, with their prisoners handcuffed to their side, en-route for the nearest police station at Goulden Street.

The design of the new police station was more akin to a 'fortress' than a conventional police station. Walls were constructed to an extra thickness and reinforcing metal plates were fixed into the brickwork. Windows were excluded from all ground floor walls facing public thoroughfares. The notoriety of Collyhurst and some of its inhabitants is evidenced by these extra precautions.

Mob violence in Collyhurst was vividly portrayed by a contemporary chronicler named Phillip Wentworth in 1889.[7]

"I remember the police station at Oldham Road – on the 'B' division – when it was wrecked by an attacking party of soldiers who came from the barracks in Tib Street to avenge what they regarded as an insult to a comrade. When the police were reinforced, I was a witness to the hand-to-hand fighting which took place between them and the soldiers across the broad road, when blood flowed copiously, and both soldiers and police fell with stunning blows under the feet of the remaining combatants. Never shall I forget the fury of the Colonel of the Regiment as he rode up the highway with his sword drawn to disperse the rioters. He scattered them as a hurricane scatters the ripe

fruit from an apple tree. In a few minutes not a red coat was to be seen. But the greater part of the aggressors were arrested and brought to justice."

The story also appears in the Illustrated London News with the "Colonel of the Regiment" identified as General Arbuthnot of the 15th Regiment of Foot Soldiers. After their dispersal the mob went on a rampage throughout the town, several police stations were stoned and a large number of policemen injured. One of the injured was an officer named Inspector Lipsett of the Kirby Street police station. The mob was swelled by numbers of out of work cotton spinners who the previous week had been turned out by their employers and taken before the Magistrates for "picketing and assembling in large numbers". [8]

In 1879, Manchester's Chief Constable, William Henry Palin, retired. His last years in office had been plagued with ill-health. In January, 1877, following his return to work after sickness, Captain Palin was presented with a written testimonial signed by all the members of the city's police force and fire brigade. The testimonial expressed the warmth and affection felt by the men of the force toward their Chief Officer.

It read: *"To William Henry Palin, Chief Constable of Manchester. We the Officers and Constables of the Manchester City Police and members of the Fire Brigade, under your command, having been deeply moved by your late serious indisposition and long absence from duty, and rejoicing in your restoration to health which we pray may be permanent, desire to offer our congratulations upon your return, and take this opportunity of recording a sincere expression of our feelings towards you for the uniform courtesy and kindness which has always and signally characterized the exercise of your authority over us, as Chief Constable, a Christian and a gentleman.*

We approach you with feelings of the most sincere regard and admiration, and respectfully beg your acceptance of the accompanying testimonial as a momento of a long and honourable connexion with this force, and the humble though best exponent of our hearts. We further desire to tender our most grateful appreciation of the patient persevering, and humane interest which has always guided your actions in promoting our official welfare and personal comforts; and while earnestly hoping for a continuance of the honour of serving under you, we are acutely sensible of the uncertainty of the time when your official responsibilities may cease, and trust it may please Divine Providence to spare your life and health for many long years after that event shall come to pass, so that you may enjoy in the peaceful retirement of private life, the ease, happiness, and serenity of mind which you have so justly earned in your public capacity as the Chief Constable of this great and important city during the last twenty years.

Signed on behalf of the REPRESENTATIVE COMMITTEE
22nd January 1877

JOHN GEE
SUPERINTENDENT

Captain Palin's departure after twenty two years as Chief Constable left a deep void in the city's police force. The Watch Committee set about the task of finding a suitable successor.

NOTES - (1) Manchester Guardian, 16/2/1870. (2) Ibid. 10/3/1870. (3) J.Caminada Twenty Five Years of a Detective's Life p.16. (4) Ibid. p.20. (5) Ibid. P.374 (6) Manchester Evening News, 27/1/1899. (7) P. Wentworth, Notes and Sketches by the Way, 1889. (8) Illustrated London News, 24/5/1843.

Chapter Ten

SCANDAL ON 'D' DIVISION

Captain Palin's successor was Charles Malcolm Wood, who had, for several months, held the position of Deputy Chief Constable of the force, during the Chief Constable's absence. Wood was just 34 years old when he took over as Chief Constable of Manchester. The son of a Civil Servant, Wood joined the Indian Civil Service after leaving school. During his stay in India he was appointed Assistant District Superintendent of the Sind Police in Kirachi.

When he joined the Manchester police, Wood was a complete stranger to the district. He was also unaccustomed to the ways of the British police. These two factors were to prove very costly during the years which followed.

Wood's term of office seemed to be dominated by a grave public scandal involving one of his senior officers, Superintendent William Bannister. Controversy surrounding Bannister began in the year 1882 when the vacancy for a Superintendent arose on the 'D' division. At that time he was an Inspector at Cavendish Street Station, and had not, according to reports, been mentioned to the Chief Constable as a suitable candidate for extraordinary promotion. Nevertheless, Bannister was appointed Superintendent, in spite of his being the most junior Inspector in the division. It appears that Bannister was strongly recommended to the Watch Committee by its chairman Alderman Bennett, against the protests of the new Chief Constable. [1] The Watch Committee's 'interference' in this senior appointment was to prove a recurring embarrassment to the Chief Constable and his men.

Bannister lacked experience and stability of character and his appointment was unpopular in the division. His conduct as Superintendent was from the outset a source of scandal, yet for the next ten years the "audacity of this bold, bad man went unchecked." [2]

'D' division became notorious for its bad character and the extravagances of its leader's personal conduct. Finally in 1892 his open connection with the proprietress of a disorderly house in Shepley Street was made the subject of a public attack, and the ensuing scandal was then investigated by the Watch Committee.

Bannister, (by bringing the evidence of his daughter as a witness to the propriety of his conduct, and by alleging that it was only as the trustee under a will that he was connected with the lady of the Shepley Street property) was able to convince the majority of the investigating committee that he was innocent of the charges made against him. The Chief Constable, however, together with the dissenting members of the investigating committee strongly recommended that Bannister should be dismissed and protested, (though to no avail) against his retention.

Confident in his vindication, Bannister proceeded against his chief accuser on a charge of libel and won his case; but the judge refused to award him costs on the ground that the criticism was privileged.

Bannister took no warning, and by 1897 his behaviour became the source of public scandal once more, so rife were rumours about his misconduct that the Watch Committee decided they could no longer afford to ignore it. The council demanded a Government enquiry be sought but the Watch Committee Chairman used his casting vote to reject the motion. However the pressure of further charges against 'D' division made it impossible to hush the affair up, and the Watch Committee finally asked the Lord Mayor to arrange for the appointment of a special commission of inquiry.

The inquiry was conducted by Mr. J. S. Dugdale Q.C at the Manchester Police Courts. Evidence was taken on oath and showed clearly that the relationship between the Watch Committee and the police force had become extremely unsatisfactory. Many adverse comments were made about the appointment of Bannister and about his subsequent retention in 1892, contrary to the wishes of the Chief Constable. This was not the only occasion on which the Chief Constable had been overruled by the Watch Committee. In one instance, a man had been promoted on the recommendation of Bannister, although he had been fined five times for drunkeness on duty; nevertheless

his promotion was defended by Alderman Mark. The witness —
an ex-policeman — who mentioned this instance thought that
"the Watch Committee's ruling with regard to the force is
wrong at the foundation of it"; promotion should be made
according to seniority and record.

The Chief Constable himself claimed that he ought to have
the right of decision in the appointment of men to positions of
trust. "I think that I ought to have all the appointments," he
said, "I cannot be responsible for men appointed by the Watch
Committee or anybody else." When asked whether he refused
to take any responsibility for Bannister's conduct the Chief
Constable answered, "I will not take the responsibility of any
man whom I say is put in a position which he ought not to
have." Another witness pointed out that Alderman Mark had
an interest in the liquor trade and should never have been a
member of the Watch Committee, much less the chairman.

How much harm one ill-considered appointment might cause
was amply proved by the loss of efficiency and prestige which
the police force suffered during Bannister's tenure of office.
Bannister was accused of shielding other disorderly houses, as
well as those with which he was directly connected. Drunkeness
was reported to be generally prevalent among the superior officers, borrowing (often by superior officers from subordinates)
was common, and had developed into "about as bad a system as
can possibly be." [3] One witness produced evidence for the
purpose of showing that the police statistical returns were "a
farce," particularly with regard to beer houses and brothels,
and especially on the 'D' division.

The evidence put before the Commissioner strongly suggested
that the inefficiency of the police force was attributable to
defects in the Watch Committee, rather than to any negligence
or incompetence on the part of the Chief Constable. Divisions
'A', 'B' and 'C' were unquestionably efficient, even 'D' division
contained "some very fine officers." Most of the charges against
the Chief Constable seem to have been inspired by persons with
an unjustified sense of grievance, [5] some of the charges were
proved to be definitely false. [6] It was true, however, that
subordinate officers who wished to report abuses in the division
had found that the Chief Constable was inaccessible to them; it
was also true that the Chief Constable, for lack of direct infor-

mation, had disregarded the unrest which he had certainly discerned. This, however, was apparently the result of a system evolved by the Watch Committee, and disliked by the Chief Constable, by which the Superintendent of the division received and forwarded all complaints and information from his subordinates. [7] In his evidence before the Commissioner, the Chief Constable was unfortunately hampered by his conscientious desire to uphold the credit of the civic authority. He was unfortunate, too, in that his appointment was made only a few months before Bannister's; his entry into the police force thus coincided with the beginning of the abuses which were the main subject of complaint. The Commissioner, in concluding the inquiry, stressed the fact that the offences were confined to one division. He thought it "perhaps not premature to congratulate the city upon the great fact, at any rate, that the large majority of the police have no complaint against them whatever." This was a kindly remark, but not altogether reassuring. The Watch Committee was sufficiently shaken to consider the question of resigning in a body, but the motion was lost by two votes. The Chief Constable was instructed to report on the conclusions reached by the inquiry, and found it advisable to be even more guarded in this report than he had been before the Commissioner. He admitted the lack of discipline in 'D' division, and suggested various remedial measures; for instance, he suggested that police pensioners ought not to be given licences for the sale of drink in their former districts, where their "old police comrades" would seek a welcome. His reply to the Home Office suggestion that the Chief Constable (not the Watch Committee) should directly control police appointments, promotions and dismissals, was very much at variance both with his own evidence and with the evidence of other witnesses at the Home Office Inquiry. This method of appointment, he said, was already virtually the practice in Manchester; if this had been true, he would presumably have been responsible for the disastrous appointment, conduct and retention of Bannister, whereas in fact he had previously denied any such responsibility.

These attempts to uphold the credit of the Watch Committee and the Police Force were not very convincing. Vehement attacks in the local newspapers prompted the resignation of the chairman of the Watch Committee. Fourteen constables from the ill-fated 'D' division resigned voluntarily, twelve others were called upon to resign and thirteen were dismissed. Many of the policemen found guilty of breaches of discipline regulations clamoured for the right to appeal directly to the Watch Committee. The council refused to ratify any of the Committee's proceedings until the municipal elections were concluded. A special method of procedure was then adopted. Usually an outgoing Committee made recommendations to the City Council as to the composition of the incoming Committee; on this occasion, however, the new Watch Committee was chosen by a ballot of the whole council, and included much new blood. The new Committee reconsidered the whole body of documentary evidence given in the course of the Home Office Inquiry, and then drew up a fresh list of recommendations.

In future, the committee suggested, careful inquiry should be made into any suspicious connections between members of the police force and publicans; moreover, any member of the force should have the right to make direct confidential complaints to the Chief Constable, or to the chairman of the Watch Committee, at the Chief Constable's office. Leniency should be extended to the recent offenders, excluding Bannister, but any future offenders should be severely punished. After careful consideration it was resolved that the Watch Committee should retain in its own hands the appointment and promotion of officers, though the Chief Constable should always be consulted. The Committee also made efforts to systematize the method of promotion, and to formulate a more satisfactory standard for recruits, which was intended to raise the average level of intellegence and efficiency in the police force. In the meantime the Home Office retained a close watch over the affairs of the Manchester police and, in 1899, the Home Secretary refused to grant a certificate of efficiency until after Christmas, the time when licensed traders had formerly been in the habit of giving 'presents' to members of the 'D' division.

In the end, it appears to have been the Chief Constable who suffered most injustice from the repercussions of the Bannister case. On the available evidence, it seems fair to acquit the Chief Constable of any major responsibility for the abuses which were disclosed in the course of the Dugdale Inquiry. The weight of the evidence given was in his favour, as also was the Commissioner's report.

By the end of the inquiry, the Chief Constable was mentally and physically exhausted. The Watch Committee agreed that he be granted a six month period of sick leave. After the six months elapsed, the Chief Constable resigned.

His resignation may have conduced to the future efficiency of the force; but it is hard to avoid the suspicion that he was, in some degree, a scapegoat for the shortcomings of others. The Watch Committee decided that a full pension of £500 be granted to the former Chief Constable, on the same terms as if he had completed his full term of office. In retirement, Wood lived at Carshalton, Surrey, and continued his keen interest in cricket. He was a life-long member of Marylebone Cricket Club.

The future relationship between the Watch Committee and the Chief Constable still remained to be settled. Wood, as Chief Constable, had insisted that if he was expected to be responsible for the police force he should have full control of it. The Watch Committee was not willing to agree to any such abatement of its powers; but it would certainly be easier to make concessions, tacitly or explicity, to a newcomer.

As the century drew to a close there were signs that some progress was being made in the stamping out of crime, though at times they may have seemed hardly perceptible. Some evidence of this fact is gleanable from the writings of Chief Inspector Caminada. He says that at the time he had joined the force more than a quarter of a century earlier, criminal Manchester was very different from what it was in 1895. Much of the Deansgate district — "that abscess in the side of a great city" — had been improved or swept away, together with the beggars and sham sailors of all kinds who then infected the streets.

Many of the low drinking dens that were the scenes of "doings foul beyond description" had been stamped out, and Mr. Caminada proudly claimed that he had aided in putting an end to over 400 of these "plague spots."

That a general improvement had been achieved was confirmed by a report in the Manchester Evening News on the 12th July 1895. "There are sadly too many beer shops and public houses in the city now, but one cannot compare the present and past state of the city without recognising the wonderful improvement which has been effected.

NOTES - (1) Dugdale Inquiry Minutes, p.96.   (2) Ibid. p.44.   (3) Ibid.p.1.(7th day) (4) Ibid. P.47-50.   (5) This was very clear in the case of Insp.Burroughs whose examination showed him to be "a man of self-righteous and somewhat spiteful temperament."   (6) Dugdale Inquiry Minutes, p.30 (9th day) Caminada's evidence. (7) Ibid. p.55-70 (1st day).

Chapter Eleven

THE PEACOCK TRADITION

During the year 1896, the trial of Mary Ann Britland took place at Manchester Assizes. Mrs. Britland became a figure in Manchester history by being the first woman to be hanged for murder at the Strangeways Gaol.

Mary Ann Britland was a factory operative about thirty-nine years old, living with her husband and daughter in Turner Lane, Ashton. On March 9th 1896, her daughter died very suddenly. On May 3rd, her husband died equally suddenly. She then went to live with some neighbours named Dixon. She and Mr. Dixon had been on friendly terms and the evidence at her trial showed that Mary Dixon, his wife, invited Mrs. Britland to her house out of compassion. On May 14th, Mary Dixon was found dead. Not surprisingly, the Ashton police became suspicious and a post mortem was held. The examination revealed the fact that she had died of strychnine poisoning. The bodies of Mrs. Britland's daughter and husband were exhumed, and the evidence showed that they, too, had died of strychnine poisoning.

Mrs. Britland and Mr. Dixon were arrested, but only Mrs. Britland appeared at the Manchester Assizes to stand trial for murder, Dixon being discharged by the Magistrates at the Committal proceedings. At the trial the evidence was overwhelming. The three deceased persons had been poisoned by strychnine. Mrs. Britland had purchased "mouse powder" in sufficient quantities to kill them all, and there was no evidence of any mice on whom it could have been legitimately used. The case of the poisoning of Mrs. Dixon was the one actually tried, but the deaths of the others were proved to show "system" and rebut the defence of accident.

The trial judge, Mr. Justice Cave, summed up in a businesslike and sensible style, expecting a conviction in a few minutes, and at twenty minutes to six the jury retired. The result was extraordinary. The judge waited some little time, but, as they did not return, he went across to his lodgings. At a quarter to eight they returned to explain that they were not agreed. They handed a paper to the judge, who told them to retire and consider the matter further. At 10 o'clock the jury returned again, still not in complete agreement. The judge told the jury that he must direct that they be taken to a hotel for the night. There was a pause, no-one in the court-room had any doubt what the trouble of the jury was. "They wanted in their wrong-headed way to acquit Mrs. Britland because they could not convict Mr. Dixon," reported one legal observer.[1]

The judge sensed this also, and made a short summing-up, tearing up any shreds of evidence there might have been against Dixon, winding up by saying "and now, gentlemen, you had better go and consider it, and tomorrow morning I will hear what you have to say."[2] The jury held a brief consultation and begged a quarter of an hour in which to escape the threatened hotel. Within minutes they had returned to the courtroom and announced their guilty verdict. Mr. Justice Cave then sentenced Mary Ann Britland to be hanged by the neck until dead.

Meanwhile the Watch Committee was faced with the inenviable task of selecting a new Chief Constable. Until Wood's successor was appointed, the city's Deputy Chief Constable, Mr. W. Fell-Smith became acting Chief Constable.

In 1898, and after considerable deliberation, the Watch Committee finally appointed Mr. Robert Peacock, Chief Constable of Oldham Borough Police, as their new Chief Constable. Peacock's appointment marked a turning-point in the force's history. Here was a man with a wealth of experience in police practices and in the rudiments of the law. He joined the Bradford police as a constable at the age of 19 and just nine years later became the Chief Constable of Canterbury police force. He later transferred to Oldham, and spent six years with the borough force before transferring to Manchester. The necessity for such qualififations had been stressed repeatedly during the Dugdale Inquiry.

It soon became clear that the morale of the force was very low indeed. Bad working conditions, long hours and low pay were the immediate obstacles which Peacock and the Watch

Committee had to overcome. Cottage rents were exceptionally high in Manchester, seven to eight shillings a week, as compared with four shillings and sixpence outside the city. Manchester's constables also had the additional expenditure of travelling expenses which were most acute for those officers working in the inner city 'A' Division. These extra outgoings were not catered for in the wages paid to the city constables, which were no better than those in most county areas where living expenses were cheaper.

In 1901, travelling expenses were allowed and a rent allowance introduced which increased the gross earnings of constables by two shillings and sixpence. The working hours of Inspectors were revised, an eight hour day being substituted for alternating periods of twenty-four hours each. The Inspectors were also released from their routine duty at police stations, and henceforth were to be employed on the work of supervising the constables on patrol. Peacock arranged that each policeman should have a definite meal-time allotted, during which he could eat his food at some convenient police station; by 1911 most of the men were able to take a twenty-minute interval. This was extended in 1923 to thirty minutes. In 1908, the Weekly Rest Day Act was passed authorising the taking of one day off each week.

Peacock presented evidence to the Parliamentary Committee emphasising the fact that police duty in 1908 bore little resemblance to that of 30 years earlier. "Then the policeman dealt largely with the criminal; now he was rendering a public service to all classes." [3]

Peacock also arranged special evening classes for the police, in the hope that such "welfare work" would lead to "the development of a better type of man as well as to the sobriety of the force."

Addressing policemen from the Manchester force assembled in the Lord Mayor's parlour on the 15th September 1899, the Chief Constable said,

"It gives me the greatest pleasure to be present this afternoon to open the first session of Educational classes ever formed in connection with the Manchester City Police Force and it is very gratifying both to members of the Watch Committee and to myself to find that so many

members of the force have decided to avail themselves of the opportunity now presented of improving themselves educationally.

Personally I am looking forward to a time in the near future when every man will be able to write, compose and properly complete his own reports. Every police officer before he can really be considered efficient should be able to do that, but I am sorry to have to admit that at present there are members of this force who cannot produce an ordinary report in anything like an intelligent or satisfactory manner. Already there are upwards of 260 men who have signified their intentions of entering these classes, and probably others will join later; but if the number who have already intimated their willingness to enter will consistently and regularly attend the classes for the next five years, and honestly endeavour to make the best use of the exceptional facilities now for the first time placed before them, (by the Manchester School Board) there will be such a reformation effected in the Manchester Police Force as to render it second to none in the United Kingdom, and such as to make it the pride of your own city and the envy of others. You may rest assured of this, that in the near future (however you or I may wish to prevent it) promotion will be made solely by examination — the best educated, the most intelligent, and the best conducted men being promoted in preference to others who may perhaps have longer service but are devoid of these qualifications.[4].

There is one other matter I must mention to you, and that is the frequency with which complaints are made against members of the force of using violence to prisoners when in custody. Complaints of this character are received so often as to make one wonder whether there is not a certain amount of truth in these allegations.

I have no desire to criticise the policy or actions of the Watch Committee or of the Chief Constable in the past; but as to the present and future policy of the Watch Committee and the Chief Constable, I think I am justified in saying a word or two. I can assure you most emphatically that it is the firm determination of the Watch

Committee to deal impartially with every member of the force, and to make promotion solely by merit. That this has been their policy is well exemplified by the recent promotions, for I can say without fear of contradiction, that more officers of long service and clean records have been promoted during the last eighteen months than ever before in the history of the force."

It soon became evident to those close to the new Chief Constable that the Manchester Police Force was entering an epoch of revolutionary change.

That Peacock's appointment was a wise one was re-emphasised during a dispute which arose in 1901 involving two members of the local bench of Magistrates. William Thompson, a publican from Beswick, was summoned for permitting drunkeness on his premises. Two Magistrates made repeated, but unsuccessful attempts to persuade the police to drop the charges, and finally appeared on the bench, out of their normal weekly rotation, with the intention of getting the case dismissed. The Chief Constable successfully secured an adjournment and reported the case to the Watch Committee as but one of many similar instances in which private influence had been improperly exerted. The Committee ordered that the report be circulated to the city Magistrates, the Home Secretary, and the Chancellor of the Duchy of Lancaster. The Chancellor refused to intervene in a matter he considered to be outside his sphere of action, but the Home Secretary supported Peacock and censured the erring Magistrates, who subsequently resigned.

During these early years as the city's Chief Constable, Peacock demonstrated his determination to achieve a degree of autonomy in matters affecting the police force. Not surprisingly, Peacock's philosophy had its critics. A number of attacks were levelled at the police force during the first decade of the 20th Century which were directed at him personally rather than upon the efficiency of the force. The most serious attack was made by the manager of the Comedy Theatre (later the Gaiety) Mr. John Pitt Hardacre.

The trouble began when eight of the market police were detected in "serious irregularities" for which they were brought to trial. At the end of the trial, Councillor Ross Clyne openly attacked the Chief Constable in a council meeting. Peacock issued a writ for slander but Clyne pleaded privilege and the writ was withdrawn. Open and prolonged warfare between the two men continued for several months after.

Finally, Ross Clyne and his ally, Pitt Hardacre, launched what was intended to be a knock-out blow. Pitt Hardacre had applied for a liquor licence and a theatrical licence which had been refused on the representations of the Chief Constable that Hardacre allowed prostitutes to frequent his premises. Evidence was presented by Police Constable Joseph Lynn and a woman of ill-repute named Gertrude Reynolds alias Faulkner. Pitt Hardacre then made application to the city police courts on the 18th October, for summonses to be issued against the witnesses, including the Chief Constable, for engaging in a criminal conspiracy. The conspiracy complained of was that the parties had conspired together to pervert the course of justice by procuring Gertrude Reynolds to make false statements concerning Pitt Hardacre. The Court refused the application.

Pitt Hardacre and Ross Clyne then published a list of charges against the Chief Constable alleging that he exceeded his powers, and that Peacock was himself a person of notorious ill-repute. The charges were sufficiently grave to bring about Peacock's dismissal if there was evidence to substantiate them[5].

There were several noteworthy features of this attack. It received support from one section of the City Council; it was directed against the Chief Constable personally; but it was also in effect a protest against the increase of his administrative power which had been growing slowly, but continuously with the tacit acquiescence of the Watch Committee. Personal antagonisms were obviously involved in the struggle between Clyne and Peacock, but the attacks had also the purpose of asserting the Watch Committee's 'right' to a greater share in the control of the Police Force.

The dispute was treated as an internal and domestic problem, the city council wishing to avoid Home Office interference – it was the Chief Constable's constitutional position in the city which was under discussion and not the question of police discipline.

Most of the charges alleged personal indecency in Peacock's behaviour, both before and since his appointment as Chief

Constable of Manchester, and also laxity in his attitude towards subordinates who had been guilty of similar offences. Much time was wasted in establishing the irrelevent fact that Peacock had once resigned from the police and opened up a pie shop in Sheffield. Two charges of a more serious nature were that he had falsified his age in order to increase his pension, and that he had entered a warehouse, on Home Office business, without a search warrant.[6]

Pitt Hardacre's case was weak from the outset. Peacock was finally exonerated, without one dissentient voice, on every count. Clyne however, refused to be silenced and kept up a running fire of vitriolic criticism during the next few years. In the end, he was forced to withdraw from membership of the Watch Committee without receiving any satisfaction.

Peacock was put to considerable pecuniary loss in defending his good name, but he was somewhat recompensed by a testimonial he received from a large body of local citizens in September 1905. On that occasion he was presented with a beautifully designed silver casket, an illuminated address in vellum, and a cheque for £624.

Returning to the more pragmatic aspects of his office, Peacock's major headache concerned the problem of traffic congestion in the city's streets. Before the era of automatic traffic signals, busy road junctions had to be manned by policemen on a full-time basis, and this resulted in a serious drain on the force's already depleted manpower. Between the years 1894 and 1904 the number of fixed traffic points in the city centre increased from twenty three to fifty six. This increase prompted the Chief Constable to apply to the Watch Committee for an additional thirty Constables to provide cover for those officers engaged in traffic duties. "The number of men required," reported Peacock, "cannot be drawn from the men at present available for street duty unless the men are taken from their beats which if anything, are too long at present, and already a number of beats have to be doubled, that is, one man has to work two beats."

In addition to the tensions presented by the increase in vehicular traffic, it was becoming quite evident that the general workload on the early 20th century policeman had increased dramatically when contrasted with the limited "preventative policing" of the mid-19th century. The Chief Constable's report of 1913 reveals the diversification of police responsibilities.

Recorded under the category of "Miscellaneous Duties" are the following examples: —

Nine hundred and eighty seven Marine Store dealers were issued with licences and over a thousand pedlars and pawnbrokers were given certificates. In all these cases preliminary enquiries had to be made before the issue of the certificate could be sanctioned.

Common lodging houses, which are registered and inspected by the police, numbered 148 and nightly housed an average of 8,315 persons. An Inspector and a Sergeant were engaged on full time duties visiting these houses to ensure that the provisions of the law were carried out.

During the year, the police in Manchester reported 133 cases of 'public nuisance' to the local authority, each of which required the statutory intervention of Sanitary and Health officials.

The police also impounded 373 horses which had been found straying, unfit for work, or where the drivers were arrested for being drunk. There were also 573 handcarts, coalwagons and carriages found or impounded in the streets.

Property protection demanded a large proportion of police time. During the year, the police found 7,825 premises insecure and unsafe, and rendered them secure by directing the attention of the owners thereto. They also took charge of 1,474 boxes of warehouse keys which were deposited with them for safety. A charge of £1 per annum was made for the safe custody of each box.

The police provided an ambulance service for the citizens of the City. The 13 Horse Ambulances in possession of the force dealt with 4,724 cases of accident and illness during 1913. Of this number, 1,335 were private cases and the fees received in respect of such removals amounted to £310.

Finally, more than 2,580 registrations were made under the Motor Car Act of 1904. This figure was comprised of 1,612 cars, 898 cycles and 70 dealers. Registrations to the number of 1,367 were transferred, and 6,191 licences were issued to motor car drivers. The total amount received in fees for vehicle registrations etc. was £3,796 4s 0d. making a total of

£17,810 4s 0d, since the act came into operation.

Despite this plethora of responsibilities the Chief Constable reported a reduction in the number of crimes reported to the police during 1913. A total of 2,612 crimes were committed against persons and property, thus showing a decrease of 51 when compared with the 1912 figures.

TABLE SHOWING AGE AND SEX OF PERSONS CONVICTED OF INDICTABLE OFFENCES, AND PERSONS CONVICTED AFTER APPREHENSION OF NON-INDICTABLE OFFENCES IN 1913.

	MALES	FEMALES
under 14 years	120	–
14 – 16 years	48	2
16 – 21 years	637	67
21 – 30 years	3179	823
30 – 40 years	2725	1105
40 – 50 years	1979	926
50 – 60 years	856	382
60 and upwards	552	158
TOTALS	10096	3463

The statistics indicate that the numbers of women apprehended in 1913 was just 295 less than in 1843, when 3658 women were apprehended by police. The largest categories of women offenders were headed "drunkeness with aggravation" with 1944 women committing this offence, and, of course, prostitution with 1003 women being apprehended.

In this year it was decided to appoint two women police officers in addition to the police matrons employed inside the police stations to search and supervise the women prisoners. Women police were to patrol the streets where prostitutes and their like were known to frequent, and also carry out enquiries in connection with indecency cases. The first two officers appointed – Emma Jane Ball and Margaret Marshall, – were issued with uniforms but were not "sworn-in" before the local Magistrates like their male counterparts. Their non-attested status set them apart from their modern day successors who were "sworn-in" for the first time in 1940.

The forces progress under Peacock's leadership was interrupted by the outbreak of the First World War. Manpower resources were drastically reduced by the demands from the armed forces. The regular force was supplemented by a police war reserve, made up of active police pensioners, and by members of the Special Constabulary.

During the war there was a marked reduction in nearly all forms of petty crime, including a great decline in the number of women apprehended for prostitution, but it is unlikely that this meant an improvement in the city's sexual morals. Some prostitutes, it is true, had abandoned the profession for war work, but a depleted police force manned mostly by elderly officers and 'specials' and burdened with fire watching and miscellaneous war duties, had little time or inclination to scour the darkened streets seeking those who remained. Much was winked at and women who got arrested were usually let off lightly indeed. "The sentences on the girls charged with prostitution or accosting," said the Chaplain at Manchester prison voicing a general complaint, "seem absolutely trivial. Girls look upon the charge as a joke."

In May 1915, the city was rocked by a series of anti-German riots which followed the torpedoing of the Cunard liner Lusitania bound for Liverpool from New York. Shops, houses and warehouses occupied by German families were attacked by mobs, sometimes numbering several thousands. On May 11th, Collyhurst, Clayton, Gorton, Ardwick and the city centre, all reported serious disturbances. At one raid a pork butcher's shop in Oldham Road, New Cross, occupied by a naturalised German, was attacked by a gang of women from a local factory and its front windows and doors smashed. The police were called and several arrests were made. The shop proprietor had lived in Manchester for 27 years and had occupied the shop for the previous 20 years.

The following day the rioting spread over a wider area. Not only were windows smashed and anti-German slogans printed on walls but several premises were set on fire. Two shops in Oxford Street were wrecked and in Millers Lane a pork butcher's establishment was ruined. In Abbey Hey Lane, a crowd numbering two thousand broke up the contents of a pork butcher's shop and afterwards set the premises on fire.

German homes were also sought out by the mobs. One house in Clowes Street, Gorton, supposedly occupied by an old lady of German descent, was attacked and the furniture set on fire.

Several policemen received injuries sustained when going to the defence of the beseiged German inhabitants. On one occasion, Inspector Tongue was hit in the back by a house brick thrown by a young woman. As the Inspector took hold of the offending girl, the mob attacked him and he had to be rescued by his colleagues. The girl was taken to Belle Vue Street police station followed by the crowd who began to throw stones at the station's windows. Peace was restored only after the intervention of mounted police.

On the same day, twenty one people — thirteen women and eight men — appeared at the city's Magistrates Courts charged with offences arising out of the disturbances the previous day.

The following is a list of the Police Stations in the City in 1915.

ALBERT STREET, DEANSGATE.
GOULDEN STREET, ROCHDALE ROAD.
NEWTON STREET, PICCADILLY.
BRIDGEWATER STREET, KNOTT MILL, DEANSGATE.
WILLERT STREET, COLLYHURST.
DERBY STREET, CHEETHAM.
CLARENDON ROAD, CRUMPSALL.
OLDHAM ROAD, NEWTON HEATH.
LOWE STREET, OLDHAM ROAD, MILES PLATTING.
MOSTON LANE, MOSTON.
WHITWORTH STREET, LONDON ROAD.
CANNEL STREET, ANCOATS.
SOUTH STREET, LONGSIGHT.
STOCKPORT ROAD, LEVENSHULME.
CAVENDISH STREET, CHORLTON-UPON-MEDLOCK.
PARK PLACE, GREAT JACKSON STREET, HULME.
CLAREMONT ROAD, RUSHOLME.
MOSS LANE EAST, MOSS SIDE.
WILMSLOW ROAD, WITHINGTON.
WILMSLOW ROAD, DIDSBURY.
CHORLTON-CUM-HARDY.

MILL STREET, BRADFORD.
BELLE VUE STREET, WEST GORTON.
HYDE ROAD, GORTON.
TOWN HALL, ALBERT SQUARE,
KEYS OFFICE, TOWN HALL.

The **Principal Ambulance Stations** at which both motor and horse ambulances were available were sited at:
GOULDEN STREET POLICE STATION.
MILL STREET POLICE STATION.
MOSS LANE EAST POLICE STATION.

NOTES - (1) E. Parry, What the Judge Saw. p.115.   (2) Ibid. p.116.   (3) B.P.P.1908 Vol.1X, p.1455-6.   (4) Regs. made under the Police Act 1919, required for the first time that a member of the police must pass a qualifying examination before becoming eligible for promotion to the ranks of Sergeant and Inspector.   (5) City Council Proceedings, 5/9/1906.   (6) City Council Proceedings, pp.372,381,341.

Chapter Twelve

ECONOMIC GLOOM

The ordeal of war was over for the time being, but the ordeal by peace was only just beginning. The peace, in fact, brought no real feeling of confidence to the city. There were numerous strikes among the industrial workers employed by the Corporation and in private industry, and the industrial disturbances were somewhat complicated by the internal unrest permeating the lower ranks of the police service.

By the close of the war, the cost of living started to rise yet again. The war years had already experienced a 76% cost of living increase. In an attempt to stem the tide of inflation, the Government tried to exercise a measure of control over wage increases. From a position where they had enjoyed a higher income than the average worker, the police were finding it hard to live on their frozen pay. What's more the ban on policemen's wives going out to work was reimposed in 1918 after its temporary lifting during the war. For most policemen, the situation became desperate as wages were pegged and prices rocketed.

Pay was not the only complaint, though it formed a background which emphasized other grievances. Hours of work were long and badly arranged. Most P.C.'s worked eight hours, split into two four hour sessions, so that an officer starting work at 6.0 a.m. finished at 10.0 a.m; and after four hours off duty worked again from 2.0 p.m. to 6.0 p.m. Thus with the exception of night duty from 10.0 p.m. – 6.0 a.m. most duties were spread over a twelve hour period. In addition, a shortage of officers and the extra duties caused by the war meant that rest days were often lost and extra turns had to be worked. At the beginning of the war the weekly leave day had been cancelled and almost all officers lost some 17 days leave in the first 6 months of the war without any payment or leave in lieu. This arbitrary cancellation of leave still rankled.

Faced with these, and a number of other difficulties, the

officers of the Metropolitan Police Force set up a Police Union to represent the interests of their member constables. The move met with stern opposition from senior officers and Home Office officials.

In Manchester, a strong sense of local grievance persisted because weekly pay was now 8/- lower than in Liverpool. A Police Union was set up in the city, and by early 1918 had more than 300 members. According to the Manchester Guardian the Manchester Police Union was affiliated to the Manchester and Salford Trades Council.

In August of 1918, Tommy Thiel, the provincial organiser of the Metropolitan Police Union became involved in a controversy with Manchester's Chief Constable. A police union member was promoted to Sergeant, and for some reason best known to himself had shown his gratitude to the Chief Constable by presenting him with all the Union's correspondence in his possession. One item was a letter from Thiel on Union recruitment. The Chief Constable passed the letter to Thiel's Superintendent at Hammersmith, with a complaint that a member of the Metropolitan Police was undermining the loyalty of the Manchester force. Thiel was summoned to Scotland Yard where he admitted writing the letter to Manchester. He also admitted belonging to the Union and said he would go on organising the provinces. The Commissioner put him before a Disciplinary Board and on the 25th August 1918 he was dismissed from the force. Henceforward the Police Union had its martyr. The clamour for better pay and conditions became more vociferous, and later the same year policemen in London, Liverpool and Birkenhead went on strike.

Manchester's policemen declined the invitation to join their Metropolitan colleagues in strike action. One of the leading "moderationists" was Inspector Samuel Latham stationed at the 'A' Divisional Headquarters in Albert Street. "Sam" Latham was a 'stalwart' on the side of moderation, and yet, when it came to pleading the case of the police for better pay and conditions of service, he was as keen and effective in argument as anyone. He was one of the witnesses who gave evidence to the Desborough Committee set up by Parliament to inquire into the conditions of the service of the police. Later, when as one of the results of that Committee's deliberations, the Police Federation was formed under the provisions of the Police Act, 1919, Mr. Latham took an active part in the work of the federation as a member of the Manchester Joint Branch Board.

The Desborough Committee's recommendations regarding pay were implemented immediately. A constable's basic salary was increased from £109 per year to £182. 10s. 0d., rising to £247. 13s. 6d. Furthermore, pay rates, together with general conditions of service, were standardised throughout England and Wales. Henceforth, the anomalies which so characterised the mid-19th Century reports of the Government Inspector's of Constabulary were altogether removed. The strike action had failed in its direct objectives, but its consequences were not totally disastrous for the future of the police.

The inter-war years saw the Victorian economy crashing down in ruins, everyone seemingly powerless to halt it. Manchester's cotton manufacturing industry had been the backbone of the British economy since early in the 19th Century, but in this most Lancashire of industries there was a particularly severe recession. Between 1912 and 1938 the quantity of cotton cloth made in Britain fell from 8,000 million to barely 3,000 million square yards; the amount exported from 7,000 million to less than 1,500 million yards.

In human terms the ruin of the traditional industries like cotton, coal mining, shipbuilding and engineering, was the ruin of millions of men and women through mass unemployment, and it was this which stamped the years between the wars indelibly with the mark of bitterness and poverty. At all times between 1921 and 1938 at least one out of every ten citizens of working age was out of a job. In seven out of these eighteen years at least three out of every twenty were unemployed, in the worst years one out of five. In absolute figures unemployment ranged from a minimum of rather over a million to a maximum (1932) of just under three million.

Protest marches by the unemployed filled the streets of Manchester, particularly during 1926, the year of the General Strike. One such march set out from Ardwick Green to the city centre with an estimated 2,000 in attendance. The authorities decided that to allow it to continue would lead to violence and serious disruption and ordered the police to break it up. About 200 policemen blocked London Road near to the railway arches of Whitworth Street with a further twenty officers in attendance on horseback. As the marchers confronted the police lines several powerful water jets were turned on and this had the immediate effect of dispersing the marchers' front ranks. One police officer at the scene recalls what next took place. "Pandemonium was let loose amongst the crowd, the jets of water stopped, to be replaced by the advancement of a 'V' shaped formation of policemen which drove a wedge into the marchers, and kept advancing. This was followed by four lines of policemen, even the most resolute of the marchers fled from the scene and the march itself became a shambles of running men." [1]

At the conclusion of the strike, members of the force received considerable praise from the public at large for their efficient handling of the situation. Amongst the letters received by the Watch Committee were those from the Manchester Ship Canal Company and the tramways section of the Transport and General Workers Union, thanking the police for "their courtesy and assistance during the recent general strike." Evidently a good relationship existed between police and public.

The Force was constantly aware of its dependence upon the support and goodwill of the general public. Individual officers were often encouranged by the Chief Constable to engage in social and charitable work in their spare time. Lads Clubs, Boxing Clubs and Playground Associations throughout the Manchester area had policemen involved as helpers, organisers or advisers. Many officers actively participated in the Manchester Police-Aided Clothing Association for needy children. An enormous amount of work for this particular charity was quietly and efficiently carried through. Two items alone testified to this — 1766 children were assisted in 1927 and 1713 pairs of clogs distributed. [2]

The Association commenced its work in 1901, and made the first distribution of clothing in February, 1902. It was in 1900 that the Manchester Domestic Mission first secured the assistance of the police in establishing the Association. At that time it was a common sight to see children ragged, bare-footed and badly clothed engaged in street trading in the city streets. During the previous twenty years, out of the many thousands of children clothed, only three cases had come to notice of the police where clothing granted by the Association had been pawned or otherwise disposed of. The problem of the street children noted in mid-19th century had, by the First World War, been reduced largely due to the work of charitable organisations like Police Aided Clothing Association.

This new direction in the role of the police in modern society was identified by the Chief Constable in an interview with the Manchester Evening News. "The Force that was once a power drastic enough to leave its mark on the minds of our grand-fathers and mothers has changed. No longer is it feared. Today it is something that has become a friend of humanity, the force has engrained itself in the goodwill of the citizens until the proved boast of friendship, a real friendship between public and police, has become an established fact. [3]

In the midst of economic gloom, news was received that Manchester's popular Chief Constable had died. For 28 years, Robert Peacock had carried the mantle of his office with dignity and pride. In the beginning he had to face many difficulties within the force, and of course without. The police themselves were somewhat disorganised, and in the interests of good government and efficiency he felt it his duty to take steps which were not always palatable to the persons concerned. He was in consequence subjected to many personal attacks which deeply hurt his family and friends. In 1918, and again in 1922, the Watch Committee placed on record their appreciation of the "efficient and conspicuous service rendered during the Chief Constables term in office." The following year, 1923, the city's Chief Officer received a knighthood.

In a tribute to "the doyen of English Chief Constables," The Manchester Guardian reported, "The city owes him much for the way in which the force has dealt with strikes – using tact and discretion and preventing undue unpleasantness – and for the manner in which it has gained the love and trust of the poor.

Out of office hours Sir Robert could be the life and soul of a social party, dancing with vigour and with huge enjoyment, and joining in mirthful games with a sort of boyish enthusiasm. Golf was his favourite pastime.

His tact and diplomacy have often been especially valuable. Though stern when the occasion demanded, he was always accessible to his men, whose confidence he enjoyed, and whose welfare he studied. Not a Constable who does not deeply mourn his loss; he was beloved and respected throughout a very wide area."

Sir Robert was the holder of King's Police Medal, the King's Coronation Medal and was a member of the Royal Victorian Order.

Until a successor was appointed, Superintendent John Maxwell became acting Chief Constable.

NOTES - (1) Recollection of ex-sergeant S.P. Ford (unpublished). (2) Manchester Guardian. 15/12/1927. (3) Manchester Evening News, 9/6/1926.

Chapter Thirteen

"THE CITY'S TO BE CONGRATULATED."

The Watch Committee received fifty three applications for the vacant post including three from serving officers in the Manchester force, Superintendents Maxwell, Lewis and Lansbury. After narrowing the list of applicants down to eight, the Watch Committee began interviewing the candidates. Finally, they announced that John Maxwell, the city's then Acting Chief Constable, was to be appointed Chief Constable. The decision was a unanimous one, his twenty-six years service to the city had not been in vain.

Born in Ayrshire in 1882, John Maxwell worked in a local colliery before coming to Manchester at the age of 18. He joined the Manchester Police Force when he was 22 and worked in all branches of the force under Peacock's leadership. "He has long been recognised as a courteous, tactful, discreet, and very efficient officer, and his appointment will be welcomed on personal grounds. Most of his work has been done behind the scenes, but it is known that in later years he was Sir Robert Peacock's right hand man," reported the Manchester Guardian. "One fine asset he brings to the post, and that is a long training under the Peacock tradition. The Peacock tradition is something that has peculiarly distinguished the Manchester Force among the Police of the country."

During Maxwell's first year in office the forces strength was just 4 short of its authorised establishment of 1421. The average height of the force was 6' - 0", their minimum being 5' - 10", and there were several officers recorded at 6' - 5" and over.

"Only the best men physically, mentally and educationally are taken on even for the probationary period," said the Superintendent in charge of the force training school, "and they have to go through physical examination before being medically examined by the force surgeon. After an educational test, the recruit is interviewed by the training school officer and if found satisfactory is placed on a waiting list while a thorough check is made with his character referees. If found to be satisfactory he is then attached to the training school for two months." [1]

Maxwell's first report to the Watch Committee revealed that serious crime in the city was almost negligable. Three murders had been committed during the preceeding 12 months, one attempted murder, three manslaughters, three robberties, five rapes and one felony wounding. Out of a total 3,471 indictable crimes reported, 1,759 were for simple larceny. "Taking the figures as a whole," reported the Chief Constable, "the city's to be congratulated on the low state of crime within its boundaries."

Even non-indictable crimes showed a remarkable decrease. During the year, 19,937 persons were prosecuted whereas in 1912 for example, 24,197 prosecutions were recorded. The decrease was most marked under the headings "Drunkenness" and "Drunkenness and Aggravation;" in 1912, the numbers of persons prosecuted under both catagories was 8,465, whereas in 1927 it was down to 3,703, a decrease of 4,762.

The general decrease since 1912 is shown by the following returns :-

1912 - 8,465,	1913 - 9,140,	1914 - 8,564,	1915 - 5,193,
1916 - 3,052,	1917 - 1,602,	1918 - 1,078,	1919 - 2,933,
1920 - 5,327,	1921 - 5,789,	1922 - 5,426,	1923 - 4,443,
1924 - 4,980,	1925 - 5,055,	1926 - 4,185,	1927 - 3,703,

"Except for the war years, when supplies were strictly rationed, the figures for 1927 are the lowest on record," reported Mr. Maxwell. "It is perhaps not too difficult to explain the falling-off. Men have less money to spend, or they are taking good care of the money they have earned, because many do not know when they will lose their employment." Whilst the Chief Constables observations may of themselves be valid, account ought to be taken of the spread of education and literacy among the working population since the Education Act of 1918, together with the changes in attitudes brought about by the world war.

Another dramatic decrease was recorded under the headings "Prostitution." The number proceeded against in 1911 was

1,299 whereas in 1927 it had fallen to 148. "It shows a remarkable and almost continuously progressive diminution" remarked Mr. Macmillan, K. C. Chairman of a Parliamentary Select Committee investigating street offences. Giving evidence before the Committee, Mr. Bell, clerk to the Manchester Justices, explained that the decrease was due to "the increase in motor traffic, which had probably caused this sort of "traffic" by women to be diverted from the city to the suburbs." Mr. Macmillan asked the Clerk to the Justices if he did not think there had also been an improvement in the morals of the city. He replied that he thought there was a little improvement, but he would not say quite to that extent. His experience of Manchester, he said, went back as far as 1890. "There was, no doubt, less of that kind of offence in the Manchester of 1927, and to some degree it was due to the system of carrying on the business having been changed."

Referring to the use of cars by prostitutes, the Chief Constable Mr. Maxwell said, "it is quite a new feature and one which has sprung up in the last ten years. It is extremely difficult for the police to prove annoyance simply when a motorist asks a girl, "can I give you a lift" or "would you like to go for a ride?" [2]

The most outstanding increase was found under the heading "Motor Cars and bicycles." In 1912, 435 persons were prosecuted for offences connected with their use of vehicles on the road, by 1927 this figure had risen to 3,215. Mr. Maxwell commented, "it would seem reasonable to infer that the present generation is getting its recreation in the open air instead of being confined to the public house, which is all to the good of the community."

Twelve months after taking office, and with a view to improving the efficiency of the force and also effecting economies, the Chief Constable introduced the new "Sunderland Police Box System," so named because it was initiated in that Borough. In effect, the system was a plan for closing the old, badly equipped Police Stations and for supplying in their place a large number of boxes, or miniature stations, which because unstaffed, would release policemen previously employed on station duties and employ them on beat duties.

The new system was first introduced in the 'B' division at Collyhurst, with the installation of forty boxes each fitted with a direct telephone line to divisional headquarters at Willert Street.

Under the new system each beat had a box and the Constable detailed for a particular beat paraded and retired on his beat and had his refreshment break in his box. The beats were consequently protected during the whole tour of duty. The new boxes also contributed towards good police-public relations by providing a public telephone line which could be used in all types of emergency, not just those of a police nature. What is more, the box could be used temporarily to house prisoners until a police patrol arrived from the divisional headquarters. Previously arrests were often made a distance of over a mile from the nearest police station, and the prisoner had to be taken through the streets on foot.

One of the chief economies of the new sytem was the number of men released for street duty who previously worked at sub-stations.. In the 'B' division alone, one sergeant and twenty seven constables were released from station duties within the first twelve months of its introduction.

By 1932, the city's police stations had been reduced from 26 to 13, thus effecting a considerable saving in manpower and up-keep. The revenue received from the sale of old police stations totalled £16,496.

The annual cost of a police box was estimated at 25 shillings, based on the cost of £25.00 including fixing, and a minimum life span of 20 years.. Clearly by adopting the new police box system the Chief Constable not only improved the mobility and efficiency of the force but also succeeded in placating those members of the Watch Committee who called for economic stringency.

The new system was very much in step with what had become known as the "Peacock Tradition." Police boxes provided a vital link between police and public at a time when such problems as traffic congestion were occupying the policemen's time at the expense of his beat patrol work.

"The evolution of modern society," observed John Maxwell, *"has reached a stage where the closest cooperation between the police and the public is essential for the preservation of the peace and the repression of crime. The old conception of the police force being tolerated as a necessary evil is now regarded universally as being utterly out of date. The greatest desire of all police officials is to assist and co-*

*operate with all classes in any and every way, and in effect
to become an efficient branch of the police service.*

*A frequent complaint is that a policeman can never be
found when he is wanted. The old police system was
devised nearly one hundred years ago, and undoubtedly
served its purpose most efficiently, but the growth of
modern society has been so rapid that the demands on the
police organisation have become so great that all available
police have been absorbed into localities of one type -
namely, busy traffic areas. The police box system will
provide easy access to police without having to incur
serious additional expenditure by increasing the strength
of the force.''* [3]

The police use of the boxes was considerable. An example
was given of a woman who entered a police station with a letter
left in her house by her husband which read that by the time
she had read it he would be in the Ten Acres Canal. The message
was at once telephoned to Willert Street Station and from there
to box number 17. A constable hurried to the canal and saw a
man leap into the water. The constable rescued the man and
arranged for him to receive medical treatment. "All this," said
the Chief Constable, "happened within five minutes."

Apart from police calls, 589 calls were made by members of
the public. Of these calls 176 sought advice, for instance, about
assaults, trouble with lodgers, accidents, missing persons, gas
escapes, and noisy animals. There were 12 calls for immediate
assistance which were met by the motor patrol. Fifty-eight
others had the help of the police in obtaining doctors and mid-
wives, and 103 required the police ambulance.

The boxes were considered so successful that the Chief
Constable reported a saving of twenty one policemen over the
next few years. "The reduction in the strength of the force does
not mean that there will be any dismissals, but the balance will
be restored by allowing vacancies to remain unfilled," explained
the Chief Constable. [4]

Further savings in police manpower were to follow the introduction of the innovatory automatic traffic signals.

On the 15th November, 1928, the first "Robots" as they were
popularly known were put into operation at the junction of
Market Street, Cross Street and Corporation Street. At this one

junction alone, two constables were withdrawn from permanent point duty and transferred to ordinary beat duty. The "Robots" proved an unqualified success and soon spread throughout the city.

During this period of severe economic recession, Manchester's Chief Constable engineered several far-reaching economies. But the most severe cut of all was announced in October 1931, the Government proclaiming that it had no alternative "in the present state of national finance," but to instruct local authorities to reduce police pay by 5 per cent.

The Police Federation protested vehemently on behalf of its members. A national protest meeting attended by 4,000 policemen was held at the Free Trade Hall. Delegates heard speeches from Watch Committee members and Manchester's own Chief Constable, Mr. Maxwell, in support of their fears and objections. But before the police had recovered from this stunning blow, a second government announcement proclaimed that as from the 1st November 1931, "a second instalment of the cut in police pay must be imposed." This second instalment was a further cut of five-per-cent, making ten-per-cent in all.

The Chief Constable complained bitterly that the police would have been quite satisfied to have made any sacrifice demanded in the interests of the nation provided the sacrifice was equally distributed, but the police were being penalised too much compared with other sections of the community. It was pointed out that while dustmen got 54s. 8d. for a 47 hour week, policemen joining the force would be paid under the cuts 50s 0d. a week and a rent allowance.

Despite a wave of protests the police pay reductions were implemented.

Public sympathy for the plight of the police was aroused further when in June 1933, a young constable named Thomas Jewes was involved in a drowning tragedy. Constable Jewes had been called to the River Irwell at Victoria Bridge where a man was struggling in the water. The man was former boxer William "Battling" Burke now resident at a local Salvation Army Hostel, who had fallen into the water whilst attempting to bring up a cat perched on a ledge under the bridge's parapet.

A large crowd had gathered on the bridge as P.C. Jewes strugled to rescue the drowning man. At one point the constable managed to take hold of Burke and prop him against the base of one of the bridge's pillars, but he lost his grip and both men pluged into the murky water.

At the inquest, Superintendent Williams of the 'A' Division said that P. C. Jewes was 25 years old and had been in the police for 2½ years. "I have always found him a most promising young officer, and for a man of his service he was one of the best, if not the best. He was awarded the Watch Committee Medal for bravery in October 1932 for stopping a runaway horse in Peter Street."

P. C. Jewes's funeral was described by the Manchester Evening News as being "the greatest gathering of the city police force for any public ceremony within living memory." More than 20,000 people lined the route as the cortege travelled from Albert Street police station to Victoria Railway Station before boarding a train bound for P. C. Jewes's home town of Chorley where he was buried.

Scores of floral tributes were received, and one of lilies and roses, was inscribed, "deepest sympathy for one who gave his life in a gallant attempt to save the life of my brother." It was from the family of "Battling" William Burke.

In the same year as Constable Jewes's tragedy, presentations were made at the Town Hall to a number of civilians who had put themselves at personal risk in assisting the police to maintain order. In one case a young man named James William Smith went to the assistance of a constable who had forced his way through a crowd and tried to quell an affray, in which a number of the persons engaged were stripped to the waist. The constable attempted to arrest one of the fighters and was immediately surrounded and hustled. The position was a critical one for the constable, but Smith went to his aid, and, taking the handcuffs from the officers pocket, handcuffed the man. Other officers arrived and nine persons, including two professional strong men and a lion tamer, were arrested. The Watch Committee presented this brave young man with a gold watch suitably inscribed.

In another case, Mrs. Edith Templeton was presented with £2. 0s. 0d. for going to the assistance of two constables who were surrounded by a hostile crowd after making an arrest. One of the officers was seriously injured after being kicked in the abdomen. Mrs. Templeton forced her way through the crowd, snatched the whistle from the officers jacket and blew it. Assistance quickly arrived and the two constables were relieved of their struggling captive.

In the year 1937, after 60 years cramped in the Town Hall accommodation, Manchester's police force took possession of their new purpose-built headquarters in South Street, off Albert Square.

The Lord Mayor, Alderman Joseph Toole, officially opened the new buildings on the 16th July 1937.

The occasion was celebrated by a luncheon in the Town Hall attended by representatives from the Home Office and neighbouring police forces. Mr. A. L. Dixon, representing the Home Office, warmly congratulated all concerned in bringing the new central police station scheme to a successful conclusion. He added that the new Headquarters, when contrasted with the old accommodation, was symbolic of the change which had taken place in police work during the present century. The Chief Constable reported, "the new building made it possible to completely centralise administrative control and permitted the creation of several new departments in the scientific aspect of crime investigation. It will enable me to materially extend the scope for research and expansion in the criminal record office and in the forensic laboratory. The creation of a Crime Information Room — a completely new departure — provided a nerve centre for the dissemmination of information, and a speedy control — through the recently set up radio station at Heaton Park, — of all police vehicles equipped with wireless apparatus."

The Lord Mayor went on to praise the efficiency of the force since John Maxwell took over as Chief Constable. He said that he could not help recalling how the ground work was laid by Mr. Maxwell's predecessor, Sir Robert Peacock, to whom the city owed so much. "Manchester," he recalled, "had known as much of domestic conflict as any city but never had it been necessary to call in the aid of the military. The police had always been capable of handling any awkward situation that arose, and I hope that the idea of the adequacy of the police would persist and grow."

Within two years, the efficiency of the force was put to a critical test by a series of explosions which rocked the city.

At 6.0 a.m. on the 16th January 1939, a bomb exploded

9a   Robert Peacock, Chief Constable,
       1898-1926

9b   John Maxwell, Chief Constable,
       1926-1942

9c   Joseph Bell, Chief Constable,
       1943-1959

9d   John Andrew McKay, Chief Constable,
       1959-1966

10b Policewoman and Police Car, 1977

10a Manchesters' First Policewoman

11a   Officers and Sergeants, 1907

11b   Market Street — Cross Street, 1913

12a   Police on Parade, 1926

12b   School Crossing Patrol, circa 1920

13a   Constable Jewes funeral cortege, 1933

13b   Motor Cycle Patrol with Police Box in
      background

14a   Police Dog and Handler

14b   Police Horses on Parade

15 Scenes of Crime Officers

16b C. James Anderton, Chief
Constable 1976

16a James William Richards, Chief
Constable 1966-1976

below the pavement in Hilton Street at the corner of Newton Street, Stevenson Square, which fractured both gas and electricity mains. The blast hurtled a manhole cover a distance of 200 yards through an office window in nearby Lever Street. One man, on his way to work at Smithfield Market, was fatally injured. Two more pedestrians received serious injuries following explosions at Mosley Street and Princess Street.

A massive police operation was mounted, with the head of C.I.D., Detective Superintendent Bill Page taking charge. Within 24 hours the police had arrested ten people, eight men and two women, and charged them before the City's Magistrates Court. One of the accused, Michael Rory Campbell, cried out, "I wish to protest against the occupation of Ireland by the English." His co-accused remained silent.

At Manchester Assize Courts before Mr. Justice Sable, the Prosecuting Counsel described how a series of police raids on the houses of the accused recovered six barrels of explosives and forty sticks of gelignite.

Seven out of the original ten accused were convicted. One of them, a woman named Mary Glenn, was sentenced to seven years imprisonment.

At the conclusion of the trial, Mr. Justice Sable praised the police officers involved in the case. Superintendent Page was subsequently awarded the King's Police Medal in recognition of the excellent work he and his officers had performed.

The outbreak of the Second World War had a great influence upon the normal administration of the police force. Existing manpower resources once again were drained as policemen enlisted in the armed forces.

Additional responsibilities were placed on the limited police force as security precautions were stepped up. The Watch Committee called upon such well-tried services as the Special Constabulary and the Police War Reserve, and in addition, they established a Special Women's Auxiliary force, twenty strong, whose main duty was to keep a watch on all military training establishments and prevent "undesirable women" from soliciting the trainees.

The depletion in the force's manpower prompted the Chief Constable and the Watch Committee to review their long standing policy towards the employment of women police.

In 1939, the force employed just four women police. Their non-attested status limited their duties to the searching of female prisoners, obtaining written statements from victims of sexual attacks and occasionally assisting the C.I.D. in carrying out observations, particularly in prostitution cases.

The force's attitude followed the guidelines set out by the Home Office in 1919. The then Chief Constable, Robert Peacock concurred with the Home Secretary on this subject, and, in 1926, reported to the Watch Committee his views about the role of women within the Manchester City Police Force. *"For more than 20 years women were employed at Goulden Street police station for the purpose of attending to and looking after the interests of female prisoners, and, so far as possible all females arrested within the city have been conveyed to this station for detention. There is also a woman available to search female prisoners at all police stations in the city. During the same period women have been employed as Matrons in charge of reception cells at the city police court, and at both Goulden Street and the Court they have done good work.*

In 1913, it was decided to appoint two women for police duty apart from the duties performed by Police Matrons etc. A considerable number of candidates were interviewed and eventually two women who were considered to be the most suitable were appointed. Their duties for a time consisted of visiting women's lodging houses, and supervising domestic servants registries; occasionally they were used for obtaining evidence in fortune telling cases, and also for patrolling streets most frequented by girls and young women bordering on a fast life. . . . Occasionally they have assisted Criminal Investigation Department Officers in detecting pick pockets at tram termini and in shops, and have also assisted in obtaining evidence in cases where girls are alleged to have been indecently assaulted.

The Chief Constable regrets to say, however, that in many respects the work of the women police has fallen far short of what might have been expected. Practical experience has made it clear that in certain classes of work they can be employed successfully and with a reasonable return for the public money expended, but for practical police work their utility is limited. " [5]

Peacock's view was shared by Major Godfrey, the Chief Constable at Salford. He said, "My own experience leads me to the definite conclusion that the policewoman would be a complete failure. Physically she is not adapted for police duty in its broadest sense, and is not of the constitution to withstand the rigours of patrolling in all weathers. It is quite evident that if policemen, with their superior strength and stamina, are assaulted while carrying out arrests, women police would be absolutely useless in like circumstances." [6]

Such chauvinistic opinions did not escape criticism from the feminist groups and societies of Manchester. H.M. Barclay Chairman of the Manchester and Salford Women Citizens Association wrote, "If Major Godfrey's somewhat antiquated ideas of women's work were carried into effect they would do away with women doctors, lawyers, nurses and many social workers, who are as much in contact with the seamy side of life as any of the police." [7]

By 1939, women were recognisably playing a far more active role in society at large, and in the war effort in particular. The Watch Committee agreed that women police, with full powers and responsibilities, would prove an asset to the force. In January, 1940, six women — including the two original "non-attested" women police, Emma Jane Ball now promoted to Sergeant in charge of the womens department, and Margaret "Maggie" Marshall — paraded before the city Magistrates Court to be formally sworn-in as Constables in the Manchester City Police.

Members of the women's department were each issued with a complete uniform made up of a great-coat, two skirts, a mackintosh, a jacket, white gloves, a cap, two white shirts and two black ties. A boot allowance of one shilling per week was paid to each officer with the instruction that black shoes were to be worn during the summer months and black lace-up boots in winter.

In November, 1942, after completing 41 years service, Mr. Maxwell tendered his resignation on the grounds of ill-health and the stress of war. His faithful service to the police and public of Manchester was recognised in 1941 with a knighthood, the second to be bestowed on successive Chief Constables.

On the eve of the second World War it is useful to assess the extent to which, during the inter-war years, the Manchester police were being drawn into a national police service.

In 1919, the Desborough Committee's report had led to the introduction of standard conditions of service, uniform, rates of pay, national representative bodies for all ranks, regular central and district conferences of Chief Constables — cumulatively these changes tended to invest the police with the characteristics of a national rather than a local service.

During the same period the Home Office built up a position of influence and central leadership through its "advice" and "guidance" contained in circulars to Chief Constables.

The old conflict between central and local government, the latter jealousy guarding its democratic control, was quietly, but notably, being eroded. Whatever may have been considered the gains and losses of such arrangements the overall benefits of the police were self evident.

NOTES - (1) Manchester Guardian 22/4/1927.   (2) Proceedings of City Council, (S.C. on Street Offences) 12/1/1928.   (3) Manchester Guardian, 27/4/1928. (4) Ibid. 1/11/1928.   (5) Watch Committee Minutes. 18/1/1921.   (6) Manchester Guardian. 20/12/1927.   (7) Ibid. 23/12/1927.

Chapter Fourteen

LOW ON POLICEMEN, HIGH ON CRIME.

Mr. Maxwell's successor was 43 years old Mr. Joseph Bell, a native of County Durham and former officer in the Royal Navy. Mr. Bell had served with Hastings and Newcastle-on-Tyne police forces before coming to Manchester twelve months earlier as its Assistant Chief Constable.

On a warm June day in 1945 a massive police hunt for the "King of Forgers" came to an end in Manchester. Throughout the war years police forces in the north of England had been engaged on enquiries to trace the source of thousands of "near-perfect" banknotes, most of which had been traced to dog-tracks and race-courses. In Manchester all bookmakers had been contacted and asked to keep a look-out for suspect bank-notes.

On that eventful June day a local bookmaker, Fred Whitehead, reported that a man had entered his betting shop and placed a £4 bet on a greyhound named "Bad Pace" running at the Albion Stadium, Salford. They money, according to Mr. Whitehead appeared to have been forged.

Two policemen followed the punter to a little red-bricked terraced house in Lindum Street, Moss Side, where they discovered he rented a small room at the back.

What unfolded before their eyes as they entered the room was beyond their wildest expectations. Hanging from a clothes rack, in the process of drying, were forged £1 notes − all 8,730 of them − and a further 2,498 in forged £10, £5 and £1 notes placed about the room.

The fantastic equipment found included a large printing press, nine lithographic stones, copper sheets, brushes, parcels of fine paper and all the other tools of a meticulous craftsman.

The master forger turned out to be a 50 year old painter and decorator Herbert Winstanley. A batchelor, he had lived alone in the room since 1919.

When he appeared at Manchester Assizes, he was sentenced to 10 years imprisonment, but after serving seven years of his sentence he was released. He returned to his home in Lindum Street, where several years later the "King of the Forgers" collapsed and died of a heart attack.

There were few notable successes for Manchester's police during the post war years. Serious crime escalated at an alarming rate and marked the period as the worst for crime ever recorded. The number of indictable crimes reported in 1946 was 16,716, a figure treble that in 1939. In 1948, it had risen to 18,459, and by 1958, the annual total had reached 24,084, the highest figure ever recorded.

Of particular concern were the increases in crimes of violence against the person. For example, wounding offences numbered 71 in 1938. By 1956, 217 woundings were reported to the police, in 1957, 270 and in 1958, a total of 326 woundings were investigated.

Robbery and assaults with intent to rob totalled 6 in the year 1938. It had increased to 69 in 1956, 95 in 1957 and 147 by 1958.

Crime was a booming industry, criminals were increasingly confident of escaping detection, and the city faced a breakdown of law and order, not perhaps comparable with that of the early 19th century, but alarming enough. The police faced the greatest challenge in their whole history. Detectives more highly trained than their predecessors and with forensic science laboratories and criminal record offices to help them, were working longer hours than ever before, but the number of complaints which each dealt with was becoming too high for thorough enquiries to be made, and they were able to devote less time to keeping watch on the activities of known criminals. In 1958, the detection rate had fallen to 28% of all crimes reported, compared with 34% in 1946, and 60% in 1939.

National prosperity and improved social conditions had, contrary to earlier assumptions, led to a situation in which crime appeared to flourish. The ready availability of more cash and valuable property — particularly in the business sector of the inner city, and in the suburbs — and the ease in which it could be stolen and rapidly transported, was a constant attraction, not only to persistent criminals, but to amateurs of all ages in a wide range of society.

The cure for society's ills lay beyond the resources of the city's Chief Constable. To become more effective the force would have to be drastically reorganised, but this was not possible until its manpower reached the prescribed establishment figure. And with few exceptions, for the next ten years the forces actual strength remained at 94% of the target figure, with vacancies for 250 policemen. Thus, the Chief Constable's largest single problem, during this period of lawlessness, was a chronic shortage of manpower.

Expensive advertising campaigns failed to make any significant inroads into the reservoir of labour. The problem lay not in attracting a sufficient number of applicants but in finding men and women of the right calibre to be police officers.

SUMMARY OF RECRUITMENT – (MEN AND WOMEN)

Year	Estab-lish ment	Actual Strength	Enquiries received	Applic. Forms Submitted.	(REJECTED)			Total Appoi-nted.
					Below Physical.	Below Educational	Temper-ament Unsuitable.	
1947	-1483	1238	853	265	48	135	-	82
1952	-1516	1233	669	437	68	201	35	133
1955	-1516	1245	409	204	30	61	11	102
1956	-1543	1320	1092	309	33	90	14	172
1957	-1542	1350	601	305	52	82	20	151
1958	-1542	1394	792	362	71	123	31	137

In line with several other forces experiencing the same difficulties, Manchester reduced the height qualification from 5' - 9" to 5' - 8" in 1950, but in answer to repeated calls for a general relaxation of entrance standards, the Chief Constable reported, "The standards cannot be lowered, it is essential that only men of the first rate quality should be enrolled."

The problem was serious, but not insoluable. More policemen could no doubt have been recruited and retained if their conditions of service had been more attractive.

Low pay was considered to be a major obstacle against attracting sufficient numbers of candidates to join the police. The

Desborough Committee in raising the pay of the police well above the level of most of the unskilled trades had paved the way for twenty years of near stability in police pay. It was not therefore to be wondered at that during this period "the police service acquired a prestige and attracted recruits in numbers and of a quality that have been unparalleled at any time before or since."

The policeman's decline from this peak of relative affluence started during the war, and had its parallel in other public services. Rising industrial wages and increases in the cost of living outstripped the value of supplementary war bonuses granted to the police, to such an extent that by the end of the war the average employees in industry had caught up with the policeman. The constables starting salary in 1948 was £4.10s.0d. per week, by contrast, the average weekly wage for a male worker in manufacturing industry was £6. 18s. 0d., and for white collar workers £10. 4s. 0d.

The differentials continued up to April 1949 when the Oaksey Committee published its first of two reports on the pay and conditions of the police. The Police Federation had hoped to secure a major increase in the order of 50%. Their hopes were shattered. The Committee recommended increases of up to 15% for the average police constable, which meant that the starting salary for a constable was raised to £7. 14s. 0d. (£6. 16s. 0d. for women).

There was no mono-causal explanation for poor recruitment during this period. In addition to low pay, bad housing was a cause of grave dissatisfaction among serving and prospective policemen, both single and married.

In a report presented to the Watch Committee, Alderman Ellis Green wrote, "Many of the new recruits to the force have found it extremely difficult to settle down in lodgings in the city when they have taken up police duties, the result has been that some of our probationer constables have resigned their appointments shortly after joining. We are convinced that the provision of suitable hostel accommodation will assist us in our efforts to recruit and retain in the force the services of suitable police probationers, many of whom come from areas outside the city and cannot reside at home."

Alderman Green drew the Committee's attention to the fact

that large numbers of serving policemen were retiring prematurely. Many of them were probationers, but there were also large numbers of fully trained policemen. In 1955 for example, the wastage figure was 139, or 33 more than the total number of new entrants for the year. A loss on this scale of trained men and women to be replaced in turn by novices who themselves were as likely as not to move on elsewhere after a brief taste of a policeman's life, was imposing a crippling handicap on a force already under strength.

In 1950 the City Council embarked on a five year plan to construct 300 'police-houses' to alleviate the shortage of suitable accommodation. The first houses to be ready for occupation were located at Crescent Road, Moston, Mauldeth Road, Ladybarn and at Beech Road, Chorlton-cum-Hardy. Each house cost £1,775 and had three bedrooms.

Single policemen were not overlooked, part of the newly acquired St. Joseph's school buildings at Longsight were converted into a hostel with rooms for twenty four young constables.

Another development which was to prove beneficial to recruitment was the commencement of a Police Cadet scheme. Twelve young men, aged between 16 and 17 years of age, started their training on the 7th of January 1953, and were eventually allocated duties within the various departments at Force Headquarters. They proved so successful that after twelve months their number was increased to twenty, and to fifty by 1956.

The idea of Police Cadets had been slow to develop. The system had its origin long before the Second World War when it was customary to employ "boy clerks" in police offices on clerical duties. During the war a police messenger service was created for young men between the ages of 16 and 18, who were employed on clerical, telephone and other duties, some of them for part-time only.

In 1955 statutory approval was given for Police Cadets to defer their period of National Service.

The removal of this interuption in a cadet's progression into the regular force led to 19 cadets being appointed as Constables during the following year. [1]

Without doubt the chronic shortage of policemen in the police service as a whole proved a great incentive in the quest for improved efficiency, and the Home Office encouraged all police authorities and Chief Constables to explore ways of concentrating limited resources of manpower on duties which policemen are uniquely qualified to perform. An early result was a sustained drive to replace police officers by civilians with clerical or tradesmen's qualifications on indoor duties where police training and experience, or the authority of a constable, were not required. In Manchester, 224 civilians were employed as clerks, typists, garage mechanics and cleaners in 1958, whereas only 52 civilians were employed in 1939.

A second result of the drive for economic and efficient use of existing manpower was the establishment of District Training Centres for probationer constables, and the setting up of the first truly national Police College in 1948.

Manchester formed part of the No. 1 district and participated in the setting up of the district training centre at Bruche, near Warrington. Each centre was provided by the Home Office under common service arrangements and each was managed by a committee representing the police authorities in the catchment area. A committee of Chief Constables recommended the appointment of the commandant and other senior posts and approved the syllabus of instruction. Recruits to the respective forces attended an initial course of thirteen weeks, which was intended to give them all-round instruction in the duties of a police officer. Refresher courses were provided by the centres and the respective forces own training schools.

But it was in the formation of a national Police College that the police service made its most significant advance. In the past no higher training was provided either to equip the direct entrant for police command or to re-orientate the outlook of those who had risen, usually very slowly, through the police ranks. The Police image for most of modern police history was a humble one, dominated by Peel's view that policemen should be found among people who had not the status of gentlemen. This was the state of affairs until the 1930's, when the economics of those years made a great many educated men available to police forces and the service as a whole enjoyed a golden age of recruiting.

During this era Viscount Trenchard became Commissioner of the Metropolitan Police and established the Metropolitan Police College at Hendon. The college trained promising young officers for higher responsibility, but the scheme found no favour with the Police Federation nor with many of the provincial forces. The College closed at the outbreak of the second world war.

Plans for a national police college found favour with the Police Federation and those who objected to Trenchard's attempts at creating an "officer class" in the police.

In 1948 the first national Police College was opened at Ryton-on-Dunsmore in Warwickshire. It moved to its permanent home at Bramshill House, Hartley Wintney in 1960. The aims of the new College were liberally conceived; "to broaden the outlook, improve the professional knowledge and stimulate the energies of men who have reached or are reaching the middle and higher ranks of the service."

The Police College and the District Training Centres soon established fine traditions of service; their value as a unifying influence was increasingly apparent, as interchanges of staff and ideas spread common standards – or, equally valuable, provoked a stimulus to challenge practices hitherto uncritically accepted.

The eventual outcome of this unhappy chapter in the history of the force was that whilst the Chief Constable struggled to maintain the number, and improve the quality of his men, the war against crime and public disorder was being lost. The grave danger, as Mr. Bell repeatedly stressed, was that the growth of the forces of crime was outpacing that of the forces of law and order.

In 1959, at the age of 60 Mr. Bell retired after completing seventeen years as the city's Chief Constable.

The issue of police re-organisation once again captured the attention of the City Council. After listening to recommendations by leading Watch Committee members, the council finally decided, as a matter of urgency, to give every encouragement for a new Chief Constable to build a strong and efficient police force. [2]

NOTES - (1) Police Cadets were statutorily recognised in the Police Act, 1964, being described as "persons appointed to undergo training with a view to becoming members of a police force". (2) Manchester Guardian 4/2/1960.

Chapter Fifteen

JOHN McKAY'S PROGRAMME OF REFORM.

The city's new Chief Constable was Mr. John Andrew McKay, former Deputy Chief Constable of Birmingham City Police. Mr. McKay began his career in 1935 with the Metropolitan Police having completed his studies at Glasgow University where he gained an M.A.degree. During his early service in the Metropolitan Force,he attended Trenchard's Hendon Police College. He transferred to Birmingham in 1953 to take up an appointment as the city's Assistant Chief Constable.

Mr. McKay's first task was to relieve the workload borne by the Criminal Investigations Department. He introduced a system whereby uniformed officers were temporarily attached to the C.I.D. for varying periods to assist with investigations. Many of these C.I.D. Aides came from the city's vice squad which was being reduced following the introduction of the Street Offences Act, of 1959 which virtually put an end to street prostitution.

Within a few months the new scheme was producing encouraging results. The tendancy for indictable crime to increase annually had been halted by the end of 1959. The actual change in direction took place the first month after the new system was introduced. Indictable crimes fell from the 1958 figure of 24,084 to 22,543 by the end of 1959, and to 22,449 in 1960.

The detection rate also showed a marked improvement, the 1958 rate of 28.8% was raised to 33.9% by the end of 1959 and to 42.8% in 1960.

The organisation of the uniformed branches was next to be subjected to review. Boundaries of territorial divisions were redrawn according to property and population distribution patterns over the past fifty years. A new fifth operational division was created on the South East side of the city to cater for the Wythenshawe district.

The police stations of the five divisions were located as follows:

'A' DIVISION — Bootle Street; Newton Street.
Ch. Supt. A. Dingwall.

'B' DIVISION — Willert Street; Oldham Road; Walter Street;
Harpurhey; Humphrey Street; Cheetham Hill
Ch. Supt. A. Bowers.

'C' DIVISION — Mill Street; Beswick Street; Whitworth Street;
Hyde Road; Stockport Road, Levenshulme.
Ch. Supt. F.E. Williamson.

'D' DIVISION — Stockport Road, Longsight; Browning Road;
Higher Ormand Street, Chorlton; Wilmslow
Road, Withington; Wilmslow Road, Didsbury;
Moor End, Northenden; Cornishway, Wood-
house Park; Solway Road, Wythenshawe.
Ch. Supt. J. Hawley.

'E' DIVISION — Platt Lane; Hall Lane, Baguley; Jackson
Street, Hulme; Moss Lane East.
Ch. Supt. A. Yates.

These and many other important steps were taken towards
the conservation and more effective use of manpower resources.
They were supplemented in other ways, the most important of
which was a greatly extended use of motorised transport. Many
more police vehicles were needed to deal with the vast increase
in road traffic and the greater mobility of the criminal. The
result was a rapid increase in the number of police cars equipped
with radio, and the conversion of many traditional foot-beats
into mechanised beats controlled by policemen in cars or
motorcycles. The existing fleet of 150 vehicles was supplemented with 26 new cars, 24 vans and 41 motorcycles.

In conjunction with the city surveyor, comprehensive plans
for keeping roads clear at peak hours were prepared, and a method
of concentrating attention on accident prone areas was developed.

Within a very short time the results of these developments in
road safety and supervision were visibly apparent. The number
of street casualties in 1961 were reduced by 6.0% to 5,269.

In September 1962, the Chief Constable took a bold and unprecedented step by hiring a helicopter to provide the police
with an aerial recognizance of traffic conjestion during a large

scale procession from the city centre to Belle Vue. [1]

It was not only on mechanical aids that the police relied in their efforts to achieve higher efficiency.

In 1959, Police Constables William Hughes and Gordon Stewart were appointed the city's first police dog handlers. Together with their alsations, Kim and Rinty, they attended a course at Birmingham Police Dog Training Centre. A recent development in their use has been the introduction of radio equipped vans, in which dogs and their handlers are rapidly transported to the scene of a crime while clues and scent are fresh.

The most encouraging trend during the early 1960's was an improvement in recruitment figures. By 1963, the force's actual strength had risen by 300 above the 1960 figure of 1,459.

No doubt this improvement was boosted by the improved conditions and pay rates which followed the recommendations of the Royal Commission on the Police in 1960. The direct origin of this Royal Commission was not concern of efficiency of the police, or about the state of crime, or the adequacy of police strength. Unlike the Desborough and Oaksey Committees, its genesis was, basically, concern about the means of controlling the police and bringing them to account when things went wrong. Chaired by Sir Henry Willink, Q.C., the Commission included in its terms of reference a review of police pay. The Commissioner's recommendations raised the constable's salary from £695 to £910, with two long service supplements to raise it to £970.

The remainder of the Commissioner's report was incorporated into the Police Act of 1964. For the first time in the history of the police, the Act attempted to define the respective functions of the Home Secretary, Police Authorities and Chief Constables. The Home Secretary was to be given a new duty to take initiatives to promote the efficiency of the police, and powers to discharge the duty. These powers included the power to call for reports from Chief Constables, to approve the appointment of the senior officers and to compel the retirement of an inefficient Chief Constable. The main function of a police authority (to be composed of two-thirds local councillors and one-third magistrates) were defined as the maintenance of an adequate and efficient force, properly housed and equipped, and the appointment, and if necessary removal, of the Chief Constable.

Each police force was explicitly placed under the control and direction of the Chief Constable, and Chief Constables were to have powers of appointment, discipline and promotion over the subordinate ranks.

All of these measures had the effect of producing a marked improvement in the morale of members of the force. The status of individual officers was much improved and proper recognition, by way of promotion, given to the value of the work the officers had been doing. Between the years 1954-58 a yearly average of 34 officers of all ranks had been promoted; by contrast, in 1959 88 promotions were recorded, in 1960, 62 and in 1961, 91 promotions were made.

A culmination of the improvements over the five years since Mr. McKay took over was evidenced in 1964, when Sir Charles Martin, Her Majesty's Inspector of Constabulary carried out an inspection of the force. He was moved to report, "The standard of efficiency was never higher than it is now, and the men and women in the ranks are people who have dedicated themselves to serving the community. They are a credit to the force and the profession."

With the satisfaction of a job well done, Mr. McKay tendered his resignation to the Watch Committee. Like his predecessor Captain Palin one hundred years before, Mr. McKay secured an appointment as one of Her Majesty's Inspectors of Constabulary. In 1972, he received a knighthood in recognition of his outstanding service.

The Watch Committee did not look far for a natural successor to Mr. McKay. In July 1966, they appointed Mr. James William Richards, the city's Deputy Chief Constable, as the Chief Constable. Mr. Richards served with the former Chief Constable at Birmingham and transferred to Manchester as his Deputy in 1959. Age 51, Mr. Richards joined the police in 1934 after working for a short period as a student-teacher in Staffordshire. In 1958 he was seconded as Director of Studies in the Department of Law at the newly formed National Police College at Ryton-on-Dunsmore.

During Mr. Richard's Chief Constableship, dramatic and far reaching changes took place affecting the character and organisation of the force.

The first change concerned the traditional conceptual approach to policing methods. First tried and tested in the neighbouring Lancashire County Force, the Unit Beat System or "Panda System," with twin features of the panda car and the personal radio, was introduced to Manchester in 1967. At Baguley, where the scheme was first introduced for a twelve month experimental period, the incidence of crime and violence fell, whilst at the same time the rate of detections rose quite significantly.

The improved mobility meant that officers could examine property more regularly than previously when on foot, and could extend their beat boundaries to include remote sites and premises.

The panda car policemen provided the back-up for the second member of the team, the Area Constables. The idea was that each district was divided into beats and each beat became the responsibility of one individual constable. Unfettered by fixed shifts and regulated hours, he was free to police his beat as he thought fit. In practice this meant that he could fix his own hours of work according to the needs of his area and could develop a kind of village bobby relationship with his own community. In short, a reaffirmation of basic police principles as laid down by Peel in 1829.

Policing in England and Wales depends upon cooperation. Without the information, the neighbour reporting something suspicious, the dealer or shopkeeper reporting an unusual supplier, the police are virtually helpless. The Area Constable became the eyes and ears of the new police system, establishing good relationships with the general public and acquiring their support, goodwill and cooperation in return.

A third, and important development, was the effect on the morale of the policemen. Their radios meant that they were constantly in touch with the police station and with each other and constantly aware of what was happening in the rest of the division. This meant that the isolation, and so much boredom, was taken out of the job, and this meant that the numbers of policemen leaving the service prematurely was reduced.

Personal radios spelled the end of the Police Boxes.* By

* The first personal radio sets were tested on the 'E' and 'C' division in May 1963.

1968 all the existing boxes were in the process of being run down, and by the end of the year only two were left. During their brief life span the police boxes had been immensely popular with both police and public. They were big enough to hold two men, so were useful for locking-up prisoners until transport arrived to carry them to the police station. Many boxes were also equipped with electric heaters to brew a constable's tea.

One constable recalled how he once used a box to lock up a small boy who was using bad language in the street. "Let that be a lesson to you," he said as he let the child out after an hour. The boy waited until he was a safe distance away and shouted, "And let it be a lesson to you copper, I've just eaten your .! .! .! . sandwiches."

The new system of policing proved to be a huge success. By early 1968 the force was fully equipped with cars and personal radios which resulted in an accelerated police response to incidents reported by the public and a heightening of variety and interest for the police officers involved. The Chief Constable expressed his satisfaction with its operation — a view shared by the majority of members of the force — but pointed out that in certain parts of the city like the 'A' Division (city centre) with its high concentration of commercial properties and its almost complete absence of residents, it would prove necessary to tailor the scheme to the special policing demands which existed.

Before the efficiency of the new system of policing could be effectively analysed against criminal statistics of previous years, the force was caught-up in local government amalgamation.

NOTES - (1) Manchester Guardian, 22/9/1962.

Chapter Sixteen

AMALGAMATION WITH SALFORD.

On the first of April 1968, as part of the wider local government reorganisation, Manchester City Police force amalgamated with the Salford City force to form the Manchester and Salford Police Force. Salford became the 'F' division in the new 2,193 strong force, with the five A–E Manchester territorial Divisions remaining the same.

Chief Superintendent Fred Richards, who was the Acting Chief Constable of Salford, moved over the border into East Manchester to take charge of 'C' Division at Mill Street, Bradford. Chief Superintendent John Tyrell, who was in charge at Mill Street, went over to Salford to take charge of the 'F' Division. These were the only noticeable changes when the two giant neighbours merged.

The new Chief Constable was Mr. W. James Richards formerly Chief Constable of Manchester City Police.

Whereas many of the institutions of local government in Salford paralleled those of Manchester, it was significant that the two towns developed separately. Surprisingly, perhaps, separation persisted when the two towns entered the era of rapid urban growth and industrialisation in the late 18th and early 19th centuries, although at first it seemed that it would not. In the Local Acts of 1765 and 1776 Manchester and Salford had one body of police commissioners. In 1792, when a new Police Act was obtained, the two towns were again treated as one, but from the very start the Commissioners divided and formed two distinct bodies, one consisting of the Commissioners resident in Manchester and the other of those in Salford. Appointing separate establishments they hence forth confined their activities to their respective townships. Both towns obtained parliamentary status in 1832 and were incorporated as Boroughs within a few years of one another, in 1838 and 1844 respectively.

The first act of the newly constituted Salford Borough

Council was to appoint a Watch Committee with responsibility for setting up a Borough Police Force. The old night watch and the day police were merged together to form the new force. It was agreed that the force's strength would be one Superintendent, one Clerk, four Inspectors and 27 Policemen. The Superintendent of the day police Mr. John Diggles, was appointed Chief Constable and the Superintendent of the night watch, Mr. John Ward, as his Deputy.

Within 12 months any prestige which the new force may have enjoyed received a devastating blow. On the 3rd of October, 1845, the Watch Committee considered charges against the Chief Constable and his Superintendent that they had withheld money which had been set aside as payment of expenses incurred by the constables attending the Assize Courts and used it for their personal gain. The charges were proven and both officers were dismissed.

More trouble was to follow. The next Chief Constable was Mr. Edwin Shepherd, formerly of the Lancashire County Force, who stayed in office for just three years before tendering his resignation in 1848 having incurred the disapproval of the Watch Committee over a number of unpaid debts. His successor was Mr. Stephen Neal, formerly Superintendent of Manchester Corporations Nuisances and Sanitary Department. Neal's four year term of office was littered with petty squabbles and objectional behaviour. On one occasion after the Chief Constable had apparently 'gone missing' the Watch Committee laid down that "in future, the Chief Constable does not leave the Borough or its vicinity without consulting the Mayor or the Chairman of this Committee as to the propriety of his doing so." Finally, after the Chief Constable had published his annual report without the sanction of the Watch Committee it was resolved that "this Committee no longer had any confidence in its Chief Constable." Mr. Neal was subsequently dismissed.

Clearly these were troubled times not only for the force but for the citizenry of Salford. Not only did their Watch Committee appear incapable of finding a suitable Chief Constable of police but the size of the force suggested that their watchword was economic stringency. In 1855 for example 79 constables were employed to protect the 87,514 inhabitants of the Borough, a ratio of 1107 per constable. In the same year at

Manchester, the ratio was 544 persons per constable, in Liverpool 455 and in Birmingham 764.

The Salford of the mid-19th century was not altogether different from neighbouring Manchester. The population was increasing at a rapid rate and industrialisation, with all its attendant problems, was growing apace. In the opinion of Frederick Engels, Salford in 1844 was actually dirtier than neighbouring Manchester. "There at least," he declared, "they try to clean out the filthiest corners of these Augean Stables. Nothing of this ever seems to happen in Salford. I am sure that the narrow side streets and courts of Chapel Street, Greengate and Gravel Lane have never once been cleaned since they were built." He was probably correct in this allegation, for Salford at this time had an average death-rate of 30.9 per 1000, a figure considerably above the national average of 21.6 per 1000. Furthermore, the average age at death in Salford was 20 years 8 months, the lowest in all Lancashire with the exception of Liverpool. [1]

The next man chosen to be Chief Constable of Salford was Mr. James Taylor who had been Superintendent during Mr.Neal's period in office. On this occasion the Watch Committee's choice proved to be a wise one. Mr. Taylor had a wealth of experience to draw upon, having served as a Beadle in Salford prior to the town's incorporation in 1844, and as a constable when that office ceased to exist.

Mr. Taylor served for four years, between 1852 - 66, and undoubtedly played a most important role in stabilizing the force during its early formative years. His resignation followed a bout of sickness which ended 28 years service to the people of the township.

Given the separate institutions which both towns enjoyed, and the strong parochial pride which so characterised local politics, it is doubtful that any sort of union would have been possible in the 19th century. But, nonetheless several determined efforts were made by local ratepayers in both towns. In 1888 for example, an association of residents presented a report calling for the amalgamation of the two neighbours. It was said that greater efficiency and economy would be secured, sanitary reform accellerated and the opposition arising from divided authority removed. "The total population of about 600,000 people engaged in the same industries interlaced in a thousand

148

ways, sharing the same prosperity and depressed by the same adversity, which is one by nature and one by business is divided into two local jurisdictions with different administrators, which are sometimes guided by rival or opposed policies and are always weaker for the division.[2]

As the old town of Salford grew beyond measure in both population and importance, it became increasingly obvious that it was entitled to the recognition of a higher status, and so in 1926, His Majesty King George V elevated the Borough to all the rights and dignities of a city.

The new city's Chief Constable was a man named Cedric Valentine Godfrey, a former Superintendent of the Midland Railway Police with previous service in the Derbyshire and Sheffield police forces. Mr. Godfrey joined Salford police as its Chief Constable in 1908 and was one of its most sterling servants, a most colourful character with a keen interest in road safety. His published – "Kerb-drill and guide for Schoolchildren" proved so popular that it was circulated in schools throughout England and Wales.

One of Mr. Godfrey's most traumatic experiences occurred soon after taking office. For some considerable time there had been much industrial tension in the dockland districts, and in June 1911, it came to a head following a strike by seamen and firemen of the Mercantile Marine, on the 26th June. Three days later the dockers came out in sympathy and so too did the carters. Pickets were employed in great force and vehicular traffic was seriously disrupted. Every available officer in the Force - actual strength 360 - was turned out for strike duty. The situation became so ugly that Mr. Godfrey made requests to neighbouring forces for assistance. Manchester was excluded because the city was already sharing the burden of the strike's consequences. Lancashire, Bolton, Warrington and Birmingham sent aiding detachments totalling 162 men.

The first serious clash occurred on the 4th July when a body of twelve policemen was escorting a convoy of lorries from the Sun Mills at Agecroft to the Guardian offices in Manchester. At Gerald Road a large threatening crowd drew a lorry across the street to impede progress and an attempt was made to remove the horses from the lorries. This action was frustrated, but the bricks and stones hurled at the escorting officers left several of them nursing head injuries. "Never before," cried local new-papers, "has this community witnessed such scenes."

Many of the policemen were bewildered by the conduct of their fellow working men. After all, they argued, by shielding the lorry drivers they were preserving the Kings Peace. However, their labouring counterparts on the picket lines saw a completely different picture. The drivers of the lorries were 'strike breakers,' 'black-legs' brought in by the employers to replace the strikers. The policemen's action was therefore construed as being supportive of the employers and in opposition to themselves and their families.

The Manchester and Salford forces assisted each other on numerous occasions as lorries entering or leaving Salford were attacked and overturned. On one occasion a convoy of coal carts was being escorted from the Clifton and Kearsley Wharf, Liverpool Street to Ordsall Lane. A crowd of 2,000 blocked the route and the escorting party of mounted and foot police from Salford called for assistance. Members of the Manchester force went to their assistance, and from 12 noon until 5.0 p.m. a continuous fight took place in the surrounding streets. Frequent baton charges were made as bricks, bottles and iron street grids were thrown at the police. Eleven persons were arrested for police assault and sentenced to terms of imprisonment by the Court the next day. In one day, more than a hundred strikers were treated at hospitals in the city. "Police Charges," explained the newpapers "were necessarily vigorous but officers generally showed a fine restraint under trying circumstances." [3]

The situation had by this time reached such proportions that Mr. Godfrey made a request to the Home Secretary, Mr. Winston Churchill, for military assistance. Later the next day, 6th July, detachments of the Scots Greys and the Staffordshire Regiment arrived in Salford together with 200 foot and 50 mounted officers from the Metropolitan Police. The sight of the military and police patrolling the streets quickly had a tranquillising effect and no further serious disturbances took place.

The Chief Constable, Mr. Godfrey, remained in office for a further 35 years. On the 18th November 1946, he collapsed at his desk and died the next day. He was the city's Chief Constable for

38 years and doubtless Salford's most distinguished senior officer.

In his first report as Chief Constable of the new Manchester and Salford Police, Mr. Richards assessed the effects of the amalgamation on the morale of the serving officers.

"It is clear that, despite initial apprehension, all the members of the combined force are enthusiastic and determined to ensure the success and efficiency of the new organisation to which they belong. Understandably, amalgamation brought its problems but these have largely been solved due to the tolerance and unselfish cooperation particularly by the former Salford officers who, by force of circumstances, were most affected by the changes in organisation and procedures consequent upon the merger."

The Chief Constable reported that rising trend in violent crime was causing him much concern. There were 1,200 serious offences of violence reported to the police during the previous twelve months, including 208 cases of robbery, or attempted robbery. The combined totals for the previous year were 1052 and 184 respectively. "The increasing frequency with which criminals are prepared to resort to violence without compassion or consideration for their victims, and often for no more than trivial gain, causes anxiety and concern," stated Mr. Richards.

The Chief Constable went on to identify an increasing reluctance on the part of some magistrates to give custodial sentences to criminals, the consequence of such a policy is that "a far greater number of active criminals are turned loose on a long suffering community. The cost in human misery apart from the financial implications of criminal activity seem to me to outweigh the expense which would be involved in providing suitable penal and corrective establishments with adequate staffs to administer them." [4]

Before the infant Manchester and Salford force could measure its rate of success, or assume its own identity, plans were already being prepared for a second, more radical, reform of local government which would create a new county district of Manchester, stretching from Whitworth to Altrincham and from Wigan to Stalybridge.

NOTES - (1) B.P.P. S.C. on the State of Large Towns 1845, Dr. Lyon Playfair's evidence on Lancashire. (2) Association Report of the Joint Executive Committee of the Association for the consideration of the Amalgamation of Manchester and Salford, October 1888. (3) Robert Roberts, Classic Slum, p.94. (4) Chief Constables Annual Report 1968, p.4.

Chapter Seventeen

THE BIRTH OF GREATER MANCHESTER

Before the infant Manchester and Salford force could make its mark the death knell was already sounding.

In 1966, a Royal Commission on Local Government in England, under the chairmanship of Sir John Maud was appointed "to make recommendations for authorities and boundaries, and for functions and their division, having regard to the size and character of areas in which these can be most effectively exercised and the need to sustain a viable system of local democracy."

After three years of investigation and deliberation the Commission found itself unanimously of the opinion that "local government in England needs a new structure and a new map due to the present unprecedented process of change in the way people live, work, move, shop and enjoy themselves." In a striking passage, the Commission pointed the way along which the reform of local government could be most effectively secured to meet the requirements of present-day society. "England needs a pattern of local authorities with clear responsibilities, big enough in area, population and resources to provide first-class services and determined to ensure that all their citizens have a reasonably convenient point of access where they can get answers to their questions and advice on how to get whatever help they need."

It became the object of the Commission to reform the number of local government areas into which England was at that time divided so as to "fit the pattern of life and work in modern England".

The Manchester district was to form a South East Lancashire connurbation, later to be renamed Greater Manchester County. In compliance with the basic principle that a metropolitan county should be divisable into districts all of which are populous and compact, the Greater Manchester County contains ten consti-

152

tuent districts.

WIGAN	estimated population	–	301,000
BOLTON	estimated population	–	258,000
BURY	estimated population	–	200,000
ROCHDALE	estimated population	–	200,000
SALFORD	estimated population	–	318,000
MANCHESTER	estimated population	–	590,000
OLDHAM	estimated population	–	230,000
TRAFFORD	estimated population	–	230,000
STOCKPORT	estimated population	–	350,000
TAMESIDE	estimated population	–	246,000

The Commissions proposals for a new County did not escape criticism. In a notable contribution to "Manchester and its Region," Mr. T. W. Freeman set out to define what was then called the South East Lancashire Connurbation. "In many ways it is easier to say what the connurbation is not, rather than what it is," but of one thing he was certain. "Greater Manchester it is not," he declared, and gave as his reasons, "one of its main characteristics is the marked individuality of its numerous towns, such as Bolton, Bury, Rochdale, Oldham and Stockport, all of which have an industrial and commercial history of more than local significance, whose relation to Manchester is tempered by their rugged individuality of form and spirit."

The responsibility for planning the structural organisation of the new police for Greater Manchester was assumed by a body known as the Force Advisory Group which was set up in June 1972. It was made up of senior police officers from the major contributing forces – Manchester and Salford, Lancashire and Cheshire – together with observers representing the Clerk and the Treasurer of Manchester and Salford Police Authority.

The area to be policed covered a total of 316,697 acres and followed the prescribed boundaries of the County. This area had an indigenous population of 2,719,556.

In a report published twelve months later, the Chief Constable of Manchester and Salford, recommended that the police establishment for the new force be not less than 7,685 men and women. This figure was later reduced to 6,628 by the Home Office. Based on the Home Office figure, the policeman per population ratio was to be 1 – 412.

It was agreed that the organisation of the new force would follow conventional lines for policing a densely populated area. There would be centralised control of the Criminal Investigation Department and the Traffic Department; the administrative, personnel, training and other functions and services would also be controlled from force headquarters.

There would be five Assistant Chief Constables with special responsibilities for crime, traffic and communication, administration and personnel, organisation and training and inspectorate and operations. A Deputy Chief Constable would, in accordance with existing practice, have overall responsibility for discipline and the handling of complaints against the police.

Following the advice of the Advisory Group, it was decided that apart from the Manchester District, the boundaries of territorial divisions should be coterminous with those of the metropolitan local authority districts. A number of advantages were recognised by this arrangement, the most important being that the police have become familiar with the topography of the district and are closely identified with the problems and the people in that specifically easily identifiable area.

Because of the population density and workload within the Manchester Metropolitan District it was established that it could not practicably work as one division; it was therefore decided that Manchester should operate as five divisions as before.

The Greater Manchester Police was therefore to be divided into five "inner" divisions serving the Manchester Metropolitan District and nine "outer" divisions each serving the other nine Metropolitan Districts.

On the 1st of April, 1974, the Greater Manchester Police came into being. Mr. James William Richards, now aged 61 was appointed Chief Constable.

The new force inherited many of the old problems. From the outset it was woefully understrength. The Home Office establishment figure of 6,628 proved to be 1,084 higher than the actual strength of the infant force.

In his first report to the Police Authority – the modern equivalent of the Watch Committee – Mr. Richards pointed out that modern society was experiencing an unprecedented growth in crime, particularly violent crime. In the five inner divisions of the force, the number of crimes for the year had doubled that for 1958, when the old Manchester City force reported its worst ever crime wave.

This rising trend has not come out of the blue. It has been gathering pace for fifty years. In all the turmoil of the present century, in the accelerating change of the past three decades, it would have been odd if crime alone had remained untouched. In the year 1913 for example, the police of Manchester recorded just over two and a half thousand crimes, or three for every thousand inhabitants. In 1974, it was five for every hundred people. That is over fourteen times as many. And those are indictable offences, not minor infractions.

New forms of crime are now emerging and old forms are assuming new dimensions. Violent crimes, in the traditional sense of murder, manslaughter, robbery and assault, continue to pose the most serious threat to society. During the year ending 1975, there were twenty murders, twenty three attempted murders, and three manslaughters committed in Greater Manchester. In the same year, 547 robberies, 3,692 woundings and 1,502 sexual attacks took place, with many of the victims coming from the most vulnerable sections of society.

Today, it is not true (if ever it was) that crime does not pay. The work of criminal gangs often yields handsome dividends, especially if it concentrates upon the highjacking of lorries carrying high value loads such as cigarettes and liquor, or upon raids on stores, warehouses and supermarkets. Such large-scale crime requires for its success the cooperation of large-scale receivers to dispose of the proceeds.

Although most routine crimes, and indeed many of the grave crimes, are dealt with by detectives attached to territorial divisions, clearly there are certain areas of investigation which demand the skills and experience of specially trained officers. The smuggling of expensive motor cars, works of art, drugs or pornographic material for example, occurs on an international scale, and has been linked with the organisation of many kinds of vice. Such large-scale organisation requires for its detection the setting-up of specialised police squads.

In Greater Manchester this requirement is fulfilled by a C.I.D. operational support group made up of the stolen vehicle squad, drugs squad, fraud squad and the scenes of crime section amongst others. The officers manning these squads are drawn from the already understrength uniformed and detective forces at territorial divisions. Because of the limitations brought about by the critical manpower shortage, many squads operate well below their true potential.

The stolen vehicle squad was specially set up to combat the tremendous upsurge in the theft of motor vehicles. During 1975 alone there were 23,715 motor vehicles stolen in Greater Manchester. By contrast, in 1958, 344 vehicles were stolen in the City of Manchester; in 1938, the equivalent figure was just 87.

The sixteen man squad engage in enquiries of a protracted nature amongst motor traders and manufacturers throughout the United Kingdom. It pays tribute to the expertise and tenacity of this team, that out of the vast total of vehicles stolen in 1975, just 1,750 were still outstanding at the years end.

Another specialist team is the Drugs Squad. Drug trafficking and drug abuse has made the work of the modern police far more difficult than it had formerly been. Many kinds of vice and criminal behaviour have been shown to be the normal accompaniments of the drug traffic. The subject of drugs has stirred stronger and wider controversy, largely because it has been affecting the young, and the young of all classes. For those who advocate a "soft" approach to drug taking, it must be a sobering thought to realise that during the period 1st April to 31st December, 1974, nine young people died in Greater Manchester as a result of drug abuse.

Investigation of commercial frauds and like crimes demands exceptional thoroughness and patience, a good knowledge of accountancy and commercial law and practice, as well as intelligence and shrewdness of a high order. Enquiries tend to be protracted and would, if they were to be allocated to divisional detectives, take them from their every day work for considerable periods of time to the detriment of general crime enquiries.

The number of cases originating from the Official Receiver and referred to the Squad through the Director of Public Prosecutions and the Department of Trade and Industry has increased in recent years as the result of the tremendous increase in both personal and company insolvencies.

There were more than seven and a half thousand cases of fraud and forgery dealt with by the Greater Manchester Police during 1975. The present economic climate tends to create more activity in trading frauds largely because banks, finance houses and other sources for obtaining capital are operating a stringent policy.

Commercial fraud is no longer viewed as the exclusive preserve of the middle classes. In his report for 1975 the Chief Constable remarked, "It is noticeable that certain criminals whose previous activity has been confined to less sophisticated crime are now turning to fraud, attracted by the high rewards."

It is probably a sign of the times that in recent years the investigation of frauds necessitated officers of the squad travelling abroad to six different countries.

The police officer of a century ago would be startled to discover the complexity of modern criminal investigation. Scientific and technological expertise is injected into criminal investigations, through the Scenes of Crime Officer. As its title suggests, this section is concerned with the examination and identification of marks, debris, fibres and any other materials found at the scene of a crime. Principally, the staff are concerned with the identification of fingerprints, with no less than thirty thousand sets of prints being received each year.

The features of fingerprints, if interpreted correctly, can lead to an accurate estimation of age, occupation and general physical characteristics. In one recent example, a finger impression was left behind at the scene of a murder which, according to the experts, indicated that it had been made by a man aged between thirty five and forty years, who did light, non-manual work, and was fairly tall. When interviewed a short time later, the culprit turned out to be thirty seven years old, a hairdresser and five feet eleven inches tall.

It is not often that the police expert has an opportunity to display his particular talents outside the theatre of police work, but in 1976, members of the Scene of Crime team were presented with just such an opportunity in the shape of a three thousand year old Egyptian mummy named Azru. The mummy which was housed at the Manchester Museum, was currently being examined by a research team from the University of Manchester when an approach was made for the police to proffer some assistance with the examination.

Using the most sophisticated techniques, the police team removed impressions from the mummy's fingers, hands, toes and feet. From these they deduced that Azru was in her early forties when she died, and that the characteristics of her toe and foot impressions were not consistent with the popular theory that she had been a Temple Dancer. Her finger and hand impressions indicated that she had not engaged in manual work, her fingers being devoid of any marks, associated with the small accidents commonly encountered by housewives looking after the home, or by a woman working in the fields or in domestic crafts. The evidence from the police teams investigation lent support to the alternative theory that Azru had been a Temple Chantress in the land of the Pharaohs.

Possible causal explanations for today's unprecedented escalation in crime have been put forward by several schools of thought. Popular sociological theories are concerned with environmental causes, such as poverty, broken homes, bad housing, social inequality and so forth; often they go further and indict the whole economic and political system under which we live. If crime is the consequence of poverty, bad housing and social inequality, as the environmentralists have argued, then we would expect that during these years of escalating criminality these punitive causes would have increased massively. On the face of it, this would not appear to be the case.

The sociological perspective is challenged by a leading psychologist, Professor Eysenck, who argues that in recent years there has been a decline in poverty and an equally noticeable increase in equality. "Thus we have an improvement in the living standards of the poor on the average, and a decline in the living standards of the wealthy: yet, contrary to sociology theory, we have a phenomenal increase in the number of crimes committed." [1]

Eysenck puts forward an alternative theory. "What is far more likely is that there has been a wholesale change in the conditioning process to which children are subjected and indeed, this is clearly so; we live in an era of permissiveness and thus have largely abandoned all attempts to inculcate standards, values and "conscience" into our children. Small wonder, given that our theory is only partially correct, that they grow up as truants, vandals and criminals, and that rapes, muggings, terror bombings and other crimes almost unknown twenty or thirty years ago are common. Even such apostles as Dr. Spock, who for years advocated permissiveness, have seen the error of their ways; yet there are still many people, even in reasonable positions, who remain under the fatal sway of Freudian and Rousseauian notions of the harmfulness of 'repression." [2]

In the nineteenth century they talked quite frankly of the "dangerous classes," the beggars, thieves, pimps and prostitutes who inhabited the notorious rookery districts in the city. Today, these old certainties are dissolving around us. Sir Leon Radzinowicz, the famous Cambridge criminologist, argues that the conditions of modern life have produced a new quality of opportunity for crime. "There is a growing awareness of the extent of white collar crime, committed by affluent professional men, business men, politicians and government officials. Corruption is essentially a persistent offence of the prosperous and the powerful, whether it takes the form of the rich bribing the rich or the powerful extorting money from the poor. Nor are the middle ranges of society exempt. The term "Blue collar crime" has been coined to describe the occupational offences of workers in industry, offices and shops, of police and other officials, thus further breaking down the exclusive concern with law-breaking as a prerogative of the poorest classes, explicable in terms of their conditions, physical, moral or social......... Frauds on the revenue can be committed alike by the welfare claimant and the tax evader. Drug abuse, like motoring abuse, seems to be a virtually classless offence. So does shoplifting in times when almost everyone goes to do his or her own shopping. Such domestic violence as baby-battering or wife-beating occurs at all levels of society." [3]

In a period of increasing violence such as that through which we are passing, it is not surprising to find that the police themselves are at greater risk than ever before.

Violent assaults on police officers, once a fairly rare phenomenon, are now commonplace. During 1975, in Greater Manchester, no less that 320 police officers were victims of serious assaults in which they were wounded or received actual bodily harm. A further 959 officers were assaulted or deliberately obstructed in the execution of their duties.

In one example, whilst attempting the arrest of two men in Wilmslow Road , Rusholme, Inspector Emlyn Watkins suffered two bullet wounds which subsequently led to his premature retirement from the police.

The incident took place during the night of June 30th, 1975, and followed a disturbance in a nearby restaurant when shots were fired. Three men were reported to have run away from the scene.

Inspector Watkins was alone and, of course, unarmed in a police car when he received a report of the incident over his personal radio. About a quarter of a mile from the restaurant he saw two men (who fitted the descriptions of those wanted) walking in the opposite direction. He stopped his car and began to question them. He became suspicious and walked toward the two men with the intention of making an arrest. Both men pulled out revolvers and started firing at the Inspector from close range. He fell down, seriously wounded.

Constable Keir, who had just pulled up in his panda car, jumped from his car with the intention of assisting the Inspector, but he too was fired at and had to dive for cover.

The two gunmen ran off in the direction of a nearby convent, quickly followed by Constables Harris and Brown. Another shot was fired before the two policemen overpowered one of the assailants. His accomplice made good his escape.

A few minutes later, the second gunman was spotted by Inspector Humphreys and Sergeant Burney. He was arrested, but only after engaging in a violent struggle with the officers during which he repeatedly made attempts to reach a loaded revolver which had stuck in the waistband of his trousers.

The third man was later arrested by police in Liverpool. It was later established that all three men were members of the provisional I.R.A. on active service in England.

All were found guilty at their trial and sentenced to life imprisonment. At the conclusion of the case, the trial judge, Mr. Justice Cantley commented, "I have been immensely impressed, as I am sure all decent people who heard the evidence must have been, by the conduct of those officers of the Greater Manchester Police who, unarmed and in some cases alone, went out at once to search for and capture these men. It is fortunate for the peaceful and law abiding public that it can still count on protection by such men as these."

Many other officers in the Greater Manchester Police figured prominently in the successful police anti-terrorism operations of 1974-75, in what became known as "The Year of the Bomb."

Hardly was 1974 a week old when the campaign of terror by the I.R.A. was launched on the streets of London and other major provincial cities. At Manchester, in April, bomb explosions caused extensive damage to the city's law courts. The perpetrators, all members of the I.R.A., were subsequently arrested and charged with conspiracy to cause explosions.

On the 4th day of February the worst single act of terrorism to have been committed in Britain shocked and angered the by now bomb-weary country. Twelve people, men, women and children, were blown to pieces, and fourteen others were seriously injured, when a coach from Manchester was ripped apart by an explosion on the outskirts of the city. The bomb had been placed in the luggage boot of the coach which did a shuttle run between Manchester and Yorkshire for servicemen and their families returning to camp after weekend leave. As it travelled along the M.62 road on the Lancashire/Yorkshire border, the time bomb detonated, tearing the vehicle in two.

At Wakefield Crown Court six months later, Judith Ward, aged 25, of no fixed abode but with family connections in Greater Manchester, was found guilty on twelve counts of murder — her victims on the coach — and also to causing an explosion at the National Defence College at Latimer, Bucks, the following week, where ten people were injured. The jury also found her guilty of causing an explosion at Euston railway station the previous year in which eight people were injured. She was sent to prison for life.

Today, with the spread of terrorism, the kidnapping of persons of prominence and the hijacking of aeroplanes, the international contacts of the police and the exchange of information, has reached new levels. The Greater Manchester Police now plays an important role in this aspect of police work following the transfer, in 1976, of responsibility for the policing of Manchester International Airport from a private body of police controlled by the City Council, to the Greater Manchester Police.

Whilst the primary object of the police continues to be the prevention and detection of crime, the demands of modern society determines that they play a more diversified role.

The County of Greater Manchester is the most densely popullated connurbation outside London with 104 miles of motorway and more than 4,500 miles of road. The corresponding traffic flow through the city and its environs presents the police with a major problem.

The motor car has undoubtedly been a great formative influence of post-war society, transforming social life even more fundamentally than the railways had done before it. Earlier the car had been exclusively an instrument for pleasure, and largely confined to the better-off members of society. Today it is used for day to day transport by all sections of society as they commute daily to the work place.

With an annual road accident rate in excess of twenty-five thousand, the six hundred officers who make up the traffic department are invariably stretched to their limits.

During 1975, 10,333 road accidents were reported in which people were killed or injured. A daily average of 35 casualties. A large number of these casualties were pedestrians, and since the majority of pedestrian accidents involved the 'under 15s' and 'over 60s', a major part of accident prevention work is directed towards them. Nearly five thousand school visits are made each year at which traffic officers give talks, film shows and exhibitions. Cycling proficiency programmes organised through this Department, led to more than six thousand pedal-cycles being examined during 1975 alone. In addition, more than two hundred senior citizens clubs were visited during the year and advice offered on all aspects of road safety.

A second fact which makes the work of a modern police force more varied than it has formerly been is the creation of a multi-racial society.

Within Greater Manchester in 1974 there were 81,000 coloured people representing about 3% of the total population. In certain districts, like Moss Side, the resident coloured population amounts to approximately 10% of the total.

The police themselves are well aware of the special problems which immigrants encounter, and of those aspects of police — community relations which perpetually cause trouble and anxiety. They are mindful, above all, that central to the work of the police must be the reality that they police effectively only with the approval of the public.

The consideration of community relations is now an element in the special training of the police in Greater Manchester, with officers of all ranks receiving instruction in the different cultural backgrounds of the immigrant population. Furthermore, each territorial division has appointed a Community Relations Officer of the rank of Inspector to maintain a contact with the various immigrant organisations.

Community service may often have little direct relationship to crime, but it is this passive aspect of police work which ensures that the police continue to win their way into the publics' trust and confidence.

Whatever the merits of Greater Manchester's reorganisation, Mr. Richards remained optimistic. In 1975, he said, "without being complacent, the reorganisation has settled down more quickly and efficiently, than one would have dared to hope last March. Critics of large organisations often express the view that size inevitably bring loss of contact with the public and remoteness from local problems. Such fears have not materialised."

After steering the new force successfully through a difficult, transitionary two year period, the Chief Constable, tendered his resignation to the Police Authority. Mr. Richards had began his association with Manchester in 1959, when he became the City's Deputy Chief Constable. Seven years later he was appointed Chief Constable, and went on to hold the same office in the Manchester and Salford force before becoming the first Chief Constable of Greater Manchester.

NOTES - (1) H.J. Eysenck, Crime and Personality. p.207.   (2) Ibid. p.209/10.
(3) Radzinowicz and King, World Currents of Crime p.28/30.

Chapter Eighteen

THE ANDERTON ERA.

On the 1st of July 1976, Mr. C. James Anderton became the new Chief Constable of Greater Manchester. He had held the position of Deputy Chief Constable during the previous eight months and was well familiar with the county's topography and culture.

Born at Wigan in 1932, Mr. Anderton joined the Manchester City Police as a constable in 1953 and reached the rank of Chief Inspector before transferring to Cheshire County Constabulary in 1967 as Chief Superintendent in charge of Traffic and Communications. Twelve months later he moved to Leicester to take up an appointment as Assistant to the Chief Constable, Mr. J. A. Taylor.

Mr. Anderton's association with Leicester was interrupted for three years, between 1972 and 1975, by a period of attachment at the Home Office as assistant to one of Her Majesty's Inspectors of Constabulary. Upon his return to the force he was promoted to Deputy Chief Constable and served in this rank for a further twelve months before his transfer to Greater Manchester.

The new Chief Constable introduced a philosophical approach based upon the first principle of policing, that the British police are a people's police. "I am mindful, above all, that central to all our work must be the reality that we police effectively only with the approval of the public," he declared.

From the outset, his policy was to take the initiative to strengthen police relations with the wider community. He was particularly aware of society's rapid pace of change in recent years which had stretched the police to such an extent that the style of policing had changed to one which placed great reliance on faster response times as a measurement of efficiency. The main casualty of this change, as he saw it, was police-public understanding, confidence, and in some cases trust.

Converted into practical terms Mr. Anderton's policy halted the trend toward greater police mobility and increased the numbers of uniformed foot patrols. By creating a greater uniformed presence in the streets of city, town and village, it was hoped that the incidence of hooliganism, vandalism and general lawlessness would be reduced. This revised strategy was not an alternative to fast, well-equipped mobiles, but was looked on as being complementary to the existing system by creating a better balance through the strengthening of the weaker partner.

Its immediate effectiveness was restricted by the limited manpower available. The actual strength of the force in 1977 was almost five hundred below the establishment figure of 6,766, and what's more, a large preponderence of uniformed officers were probationer constables. "Unlike the period when I was a constable," commented Mr. Anderton, "when there was a preponderence of experienced officers, today the great majority of constables on operational patrol in the uniformed branches are probationers with less than two years service. Three thousand of my constables are engaged on foot patrol duties and one thousand four hundred of them have less than three years service. A further four hundred and fifty have between three and five years service. Over one thousand of these foot patrol constables are under twenty-three years of age. The basic responsibility for preserving law and order in the streets of an urban area of three million inhabitants is, therefore, in very young hands. They do an excellent job, but I sometimes wonder if their difficulties are fully appreciated by the public."

Underpinning this approach to modern policing is the view that the general public play an important role in the stand against lawlessness and decadence in society. The willingness of victims to report crimes and the preparedness of civilians to become involved in the detection and apprehension of offenders are but two examples illustrating the crucial involvement of the community. In a recent study of response times, [1] it was revealed that police reaction to a crime of violence was most swift, three plus minutes, whereas the delay in reporting by victims was greatest, sixty plus minutes. Anderton's concept of preventative policing therefore aims to bring about an improvement in those factors which lead to a reduction in the community's reticence and reluctance to report crime.

It cannot be denied that the reactive and detective elements in the force are themselves crucial to the success of this policy, since any police system must be capable of dealing with, and solving, the major issues if it is to retain its credibility.

The statistics and variations in crime for 1977 are not dissimilar from those for 1976, or even the previous year, but they still represent an intolerable level of violence. Expressing his grave concern over this violent strain in the commission of crime, the Chief Constable stated, *"What we are witnessing today in my area and many others is a wave of senseless violence leaving in its wake too many wrecked lives. The true measure of the problem is not to be found in statistics but in the homes of innocent victims who have suffered at the hands of cruel thugs, and in the casualty departments of hospitals where victims are being treated for their injuries. For the offender, the crime may be no more than a flash of violent actions which he conveniently puts out of his mind when it is all over; but for the unfortunate victim, it can be a haunting memory of fear, or a torment of terror that lingers for a very long time. Nor does the drama in our Courts reflect the real gravity of the situation. It is about time we all woke-up to the fact that we are simply not succeeding in our bid to substantially reduce the amount of violent crime."*

Mr. Anderton recognised that if confidence in the police was to be upheld and, in some cases, reaffirmed, then for their part the police must display an openness and frankness which hitherto had not been very much in evidence. This notion of "public accountability" called forth a responsive working relationship with representatives of the press, radio and television networks, *"I believe the public are, within certain limits, perfectly entitled to know what sort of police force they have working for them and what we are doing. It is no good us – the police – setting ourselves up mightily as defenders, custodians and saviours of the people, seeking to inspire public confidence and support and then skulking unnecessarily behind a flimsy veil of secrecy everytime we are duly asked for information or to account for our conduct. Such practices are bound to lead to suspicion and mistrust and*

lend force to our enemies. Continuous police reticence will be regarded at best as doubt of our own ability and at worst perhaps as deliberate evasion. There can be nothing more harmful to the police than a news-starved and ill-informed public feeding on rumour and speculation." [2]
Any policy which makes explicit an adherence to the principles of "openness and frankness" will, I feel sure, make the task of the future historian a good deal lighter than the barren ground of secrecy that was police history up to the present day.

NOTES - (1) Dr. M. Punch, The Police and their Publics, Discussion Paper delivered at Cranfield Institute 1977.   (2) Chief Constable's Annual Report 1977.

CHIEF CONSTABLES OF MANCHESTER

CAPTAIN EDWARD WILLIS.	1842 – 1857
CAPTAIN WILLIAM HENRY PALIN.	1857 – 1880
CHARLES MALCOLM WOOD.	1881 – 1896
W. FELL-SMITH (Acting).	1897 – 1898
ROBERT PEACOCK.	1898 – 1926
JOHN MAXWELL.	1927 – 1943
JOSEPH BELL.	1943 – 1958
JOHN ANDREW McKAY.	1958 – 1966
WILLIAM JAMES RICHARDS.	1966 – 1968
Manchester and Salford	1968 – 1974
Greater Manchester Police	1974 – 1976
C. JAMES ANDERTON.	1976 –

LANCASHIRE POLICE FORCES 1836 – 1856

NAME OF FORCE	DATE OF INAUGURA- TION	POPULATION	INITIAL ESTABLI- -SHMENT
Lancashire County Constabulary	1839	995,301(1841)	502
Borough Forces:- Lancaster	1824	10,144(1821)	9
Wigan	1836	20,774(1831)	6
Liverpool	1836	205,954(1831)	290
Preston	1836	36,336(1831)	7
Manchester	1842	242,983(1841)	398
Bolton	1842	49,763(1841)	22
Salford	1844	53,200(1841)	31
Warrington	1847	22,894(1851) (after reorganisation in 1838)	5
Ashton	1848	30,676(1851)	13
Oldham	1849	52,820(1851)	12
Blackburn	1852	46,536(1851)	12

APPENDIX C

MANCHESTER POLICE DISTRICTS – 1839

NAMES AND BOUNDARIES OF THE POLICE DISTRICTS OF MANCHESTER

No. 1. NEW CROSS DISTRICT, bounded by the New Cross and Great Ancoats-street, Oldham-road, and the River Medlock.

No. 2. ST MICHAEL'S DISTRICT, bounded by Oldham-street, Swan-street, Miller street, part of Long Millgate, to Scotland bridge and along the river Irk.

No. 3. COLLEGIATE CHURCH DISTRICT, bounded by Scotland bridge, and part of Long Millgate, to and through Miller-street, by Shudehill, Hanging-ditch, Cateaton-street, down to Salford bridge, the river Irwell, and the North-side of the said Church.

No. 4. ST CLEMENT'S DISTRICT, bounded by Great Ancoats-street, Lever-street and the river Medlock.

No. 5. ST.PAUL'S DISTRICT, bounded by Lever-street,New Cross, Swan-street, Shudehill, Nicholas Croft, High-Street, Market-street and Piccadilly.

No. 6. EXCHANGE DISTRICT, bounded by Market-street, St. Mary's-gate, Deansgate, Cateaton-street, Hanging ditch, Withygrove, Nicholas-croft and High-Street.

No. 7. MINSHULL DISTRICT, bounded by Piccadilly, London-road, Portland-street, Brook-street, and the river Medlock.

No. 8.   ST. JAMES'S DISTRICT, bounded by Piccadilly, Portland-street, Bond-street, and Fountain-street.

No. 9.   ST. ANN'S DISTRICT, bounded by St. Mary-gate, Market-street, Fountain-street, Brazennose-street, Princess-street and Deansgate.

No. 10. OXFORD-STREET DISTRICT, bounded by Bond-street, Brook-street, Mosley-street and the river Medlock.

No. 11. ST. PETER'S DISTRICT, bounded by Mosley-street the river Medlock, Deansgate, Brazennose-street, and Princess-street.

No. 12   ST. MARY'S DISTRICT, bounded by Old Bridge-street, Deansgate, Bridge-street and the river Irwell.

No. 13. OLD QUAY DISTRICT, bounded by Bridge-street, Deansgate, Quay-street and the river Irwell.

No. 14. ST. JOHN'S DISTRICT, bounded by Quay-street, Deansgate, the Canal, the river Medlock, and the river Irwell.

LIST OF ALL OFFICERS AND MEN SERVING IN THE MANCHESTER CITY POLICE ONE HUNDRED YEARS AGO

22nd JANUARY 1877

CHIEF CONSTABLE
Captain William Henry Palin

DEPUTY CHIEF CONSTABLE
Captain Thomas Angelo Irwin

A   DIVISION

SUPERINTENDENT
John Gee

INSPECTORS

1.	James Cahill	4.	James Matthews
2.	Charles Carlisle	5.	James Hartley
3.	Andrew Drysdale	6.	Joseph Simpson

SERGEANTS

1.	Ephraim Brears	7.	James Burgess
2.	William Rushworth	8.	Richard Siddorn
3.	James Taylor	9.	George Goodwin
4.	Joseph Wolfenden	10.	Bramley Buckley
5.	Henry Robinson	11.	John Smith
6.	Alfred Bruce		

CONSTABLES

1. Edred Booth
2. James Thompson
3. Charles Schofield
4. James Challinor
5. Hugh D. Reynolds
6. William McDonald
7. John Verner
8. Joshua Sykes
9. John Jackson
10. John Sutton
11. William J. Pope
12. William Cockcroft
13. Thomas Redfern
14. John Lincoln
15. John Thompson
16. Henry Woodgett
17. George Smith
18. Albert C.Griffett
19. Charles Broomhall
20. George McCormick
21. Samuel Wray
22. William Murray
23. William Bonney
24. James Bramley
25. John Phipps
26. William Schofield
27. Joseph Blanning
28. Joseph Higgins
29. John Rhodes
30. Edward Lomas
31. Thomas Brandon
32. William Gresswell
33. Ralph Critchlow
34. Adolphus Galbraith
35. Thomas Dunnicliffe
36. Joseph Burbridge
37. John Hy. Astington
38. Henry W. Bayley
39. William Hanton
40. William Cole
41. Joseph Hardishy
42. William Faulkner
43. John Rustage
44. Thomas Allman
45. George Wilford
46. John Bailey
47. John Stubbs
48. James Kelsall
49. James Hanlon
50. John Wheeldon
51. Peter Gillespie
52. Thomas Gibson
53. Leonard Greenwood
54. Randal Sykes
55. John Lane
56. Abel Heath
57. Richard Talbot
58. William France
59. James Dark
60. Walter Brook
61. David Lomas
63. Allen Durrans
64. John Grundy
65. William H. Nicholls
66. James McDonald
67. William Townsend
68. Thomas Crawford
69. Joseph Lilly

70. Thomas Tomlinson
71. William Grice
72. Samuel Turner
74. Henry Flake
75. Thomas Brennon
76. William Trueman
77. Daniel Royle
78. John Stoney
79. John Plumb
80. John Day
81. Christr. McCormick
82. Charles Hunt
83. George Williams
84. Edward Wood
85. James Beard
86. James Wright
87. John Cooper
88. Robert Stephens
89. Charles Perrin
90. Thomas Hope
91. Alexander Frazer
92. William Gray
93. John Ruddick
94. Henry Woods
95. James Melling
96. Joseph Mullins
97. Robert Moreland
98. John Honan
99. Daniel Lincoln
100. John Kerr
101. Joseph Ward
102. Joseph Nadin
103. Mark Harrison
104. William O'Neill
105. Donald McLean
106. Thomas G. Jones
107. Anthony Oliver
108. James Preston
109. William Lennon
110. John Murchison

111. Thomas Nicklin
112. John Brady
113. James Bentley
114. John Mason
115. Murdoch Bain
116. Peter Marnock
118. William Linter
119. Samuel Ingham
120. Samuel Cluer
121. John Henry Gordon
122. William Kennedy
123. George Jackson
124. William Waltho
125. Richard Watson
126. William Leigh
127. Walter Cox
128. Samuel Weller
129. Ingham Smith
130. John Oulton
131. James Densham
132. Enoch Wilkinson
133. George Hills
134. John W. Clowes
135. William Hughes
136. Henry Snowdon
137. William Rothwell
138. James Swindells
139. John Bell
140. William McDowell
141. Charles Bradbury
142. James Brocklehurst
143. James Taylor
144. Ralph Frith
145. William Gardiner
146. Thomas Williams
147. William Dickinson
148. Thomas Marnock
149. Thomas Cheetham
150. Edwin Wheeler
152. John Day

174

153. Andrew Hallett
154. Thomas Tuckey
155. William Forrie
156. Robert Stansfield
157. John P. Doran
158. Peter W. Pezet
159. George Watson
160. John Walton
161. Robert Stephens
162. Jonathan Grant
163. Edward Nuthall
164. William R. Hills
165. Thomas Thomlinson
166. Samual Staton
167. George Wilson
168. George Winn
169. Isaac Smethurst
170. James Durkin

171. Harry Gault
172. Thomas Cordon
173. William Durham
174. Robert Clayton
175. Edward Kennedy
176. John Granleese
177. John Lowe
178. George Phillips
179. John Harding
180. Alexander Fraser
181. Thomas Atherton
182. George Snell
183. Mark Langdon
184. Richard Rushby
185. Valentine Hughes
186. Henry Marshall
196. Hugh Ryan

B DIVISION

SUPERINTENDENT

Charles William Godby

INSPECTORS

1. Thomas Wilson
2. Ezekiel Potts
3. Frederick Holland
4. William Wilde
5. Thomas Barber
6. Richard Hutchinson

SERGEANTS

1. Henry Lightfoot
2. Hugh Helm
3. John Brindley
4. James Dean
5. George Bailey
6. Robert Potts
7. Oates Riley
8. Charles Crowther
9. James Chambers
10. Joseph Goodwin
11. Joseph Barnes

CONSTABLES

1. Henry Newton
2. Thomas Adkins
3. Samuel Dean
4. John Hazlehurst
5. Charles James
6. Joseph Crompton
7. James Simpson
8. Francis Harris
9. William Ellison
10. William Doughty
11. William Whiteley
12. William Fiddeman

13. Ambrose Williams
14. James Brook
15. William Burke
16. Richard Etchells
17. James Hy. Dickerson
18. Joseph W. Prior
19. Job Bradburn
20. William Temple
21. John Henry Jones
22. Andrew Dick
23. William Geo. Hill
24. William Delaney
26. Thomas Wright
27. Benjamin Tomlinson
28. Robert Hastings
29. Paul Hambleton
30. Richard Williams
31. John Johnson
32. Joseph Pilsbury
33. Henry Stott
34. William Horsfield
35. William Reeves
36. Joseph Schofield
37. Thomas McMahon
38. William Stowell
39. John Cunnane
40. Reuben Gray
41. Richard Stead
42. Joseph Kirkman
43. William Gibbons
44. William Bell
45. Robert Heywood
46. George Robinson
47. Thomas Hyde
48. Henry Greenwood
49. George Warrender
50. David McCliments
51. Robert Johnston
52. Thomas Hogg
53. Thomas Bond

54. William Patterson
55. Denis Murphy
56. James Eyre
57. James Jarman
59. William J. Hanlon
60. Thomas Goodwin
61. Eli Blackmore
62. John Hillier
63. Henry Green
64. Edward Mason
65. Josiah Sanders
66. Thomas Grantham
67. Thomas Lambert
68. William Gaskell
69. Robert Thompson
70. Joseph Hibbert
71. Michael Nolan
72. William Fox
73. George Broom
75. George Bowe
76. Charles Rowbotham
77. John Hobson
78. Iabez Sykes
79. David Gibson
80. George Walker
81. Henry Burton
82. Denis O'Sullivan
83. James Livingstone
84. John Morley
85. George Clarke
86. James Keith
87. John Morris
88. Ebenezer Phipps
89. Samuel Howles
90. Richard Ashworth
91. James Clark
92. Samuel Bicknell
93. Thomas Tomlinson
94. Henry Fahy
95. Thomas Barber

96. William Hayes
97. Alfred C. Smith
98. Thomas Vickery
99. Fracis Butler
100. Henry Groves
101. Enoch Batkin
102. William Coates
103. Samuel Thorpe
104. Edward Heathcote
105. Henry Atkin
106. Charles Wade
107. Patrick Coleman
108. Thomas Brunt
109. Henry Valentine
110. Robert Plymsell
111. John Wurm
112. Joseph Sutton
113. William Dunhill
114. Adam R. Coates
115. Joseph Sherriff
116. Thomas Staples
117. Josiah Harper
118. William Turner
119. Thomas King
120. William Mellor
121. John Crabtree
122. John Bassett
123. John Peake
124. Robert J. Allen
125. William Sherwin
126. Richard Dorricott

127. Richard Blackney
128. Michael Jackson
129. William Skimming
130. John Palmer
131. Fracis Harding
132. John Tomlinson
133. Henry Johnson
134. James Warburton
135. William Bridges
136. William Creer
137. John Beverley
138. Joseph Jackson
139. Thomas Gelseman
140. John Murray
141. Apollos Allison
142. Archibald McKinley
143. George Hardy
144. Alexander Grant
145. James T. Ling
146. John Mawson
147. John Mills
149. William Dale
150. Enoch Hewitt
151. Thomas Davies
152. Richard Whaley
153. Patrick Denash
156. Joseph W. Hunter
158. Henry Ferris
161. Joseph Pape
165. John Doughty

C DIVISION

SUPERINTENDENT

Thomas Anderton

INSPECTORS

1. Joseph Horner
2. James Woodward
3. James C. Long
4. Ralph Rowbottom
5. William Leech
6. Thomas Pigott

SERGEANTS

1. John Gresty
2. Jonathan Davenport
3. Thomas Taylor
4. James Heap
5. Jacob Bairstow
6. Francis Sheriden
7. James Fisher
8. Joseph Steele
9. Thomas Martin
10. William Bannister
11. Thomas Grantham

CONSTABLES

2. Edward Corbett
3. John Gallop
4. William Grubb
5. William Wild
6. Robert Beswick
7. Henry Thornton
8. George Twigg
9. Nicholas Weeks
10. Reuben Smith
11. Peter Burton
12. Walter Shirley
13. James Sumner

14.	Edwin Southwick	56.	John Atkin
15.	Henry Holland	57.	George Ladd
16.	Wright Whitehead	58.	Charles Parnell
17.	Isaac Ambler	59.	Thomas Brady
18.	Lewis Cameron	60.	Thomas Fagan
19.	Thomas Bradbury	61.	Terence Boyle
20.	James Taylor	62.	William Dawson
21.	William Howard	63.	Alexander H. Browning
22.	William Clayton	64.	William McCredie
23.	Nicholas Oxley	65.	James Jackson
24.	Charles Field	66.	James Brady
25.	Henry Fletcher	67.	James Kane
26.	Edwin Walker	68.	George C. White
27.	George Bailey	69.	David Lovell
28.	Thomas Holland	70.	Robert Saville
29.	James Thomas	71.	John Kelly
30.	George Durrant	72.	Abraham Harrison
31.	Henry Moreland	73.	George Warren
32.	Abraham Bradley	74.	Samuel Lowe
33.	David Cocking	75.	Fred Birds
34.	John Evans	76.	Henry Allcock
35.	Thomas Sloane	77.	David Warren
36.	Enoch Snowden	78.	James Nicholls
37.	William T. Dawson	79.	Christopher Nicholson
38.	SquireTrippier	80.	William Askew
41.	John Walker	81.	William Mastin
42.	Isaac Leah	82.	William Webber
43.	Henry Hazlehurst	83.	Charles Bowcott
44.	Joseph Iles	84.	James Horn
45.	William Abel	85.	Thomas Beresford
46.	George Edwards	86.	Ben W. Horn
47.	Thomas Froggatt	87.	Tom Samways
48.	Charles Pettengale	88.	William Willett
49.	Robert Davidson	89.	William Ritchie
50.	Henry Gratton	90.	John Foster
51.	Thomas Tyler	91.	Joseph Bailey
52.	John Benson	92.	John I. Bell
53.	James Lawton	93.	John Ashworth
54.	James Pownall	94.	Christopher Read
55.	James Wild	95.	Matthew Jackson

96. Henry Valentine
98. William Bowness
99. Joseph Tomkinson
100. Thomas Godfrey
101. William Milverton
102. George Parker
103. Peter Greer
104. John Braddock
105. John Andrews
106. John Maver
107. Christopher Allbrook
108. John W. Steele
110. John Ruby
111. William Lowe
112. Joseph Stafford
113. Charles Summers
114. Henry Baker
115. George W. Ash
116. George Bowers
117. Thomas Chetwood
118. James Shaw
119. James Martland
120. George Rawlinson
121. Tom Strend
122. Charles Morton
123. Robert Critchlow
124. Edward Birch

125. John Jackson
126. George Swinburn
127. Henry Paddon
128. William Veale
129. Charles Walker
130. John Hallworth
131. Jesse Porter
132. John Thomas
133. Daniel Wagstaff
134. Fred Middleton
135. John Ratcliffe
136. Alfred Tomkinson
137. Wm.E. Broderick
138. Thomas Bates
139. William Pett
140. George Girdham
141. Albert Cavell
142. Joseph Nixon
143. George Harlow
144. Samuel Chetwood
145. Henry Caiger
146. Walter T. Tomlinson
147. John Pillinger
150. Benjamin Galbraith
151. Thomas Wilson
153. John Wright
155 William Card
156. Walter Boshvick

D   D I V I S I O N

SUPERINTENDENT

Thomas Meade

INSPECTORS

1. Joseph Arlom
2. James Labert
3. William Harrop
4. John Greatorex
5. John Orme
6. Robert Brown

SERGEANTS

1. William Armstrong
2. Edward Wheeler
3. John Wilkinson
4. George Holland
5. Robert Brown
6. John Robinson
7. Samuel Burroughs
8. James Grice
9. Joseph Potts
10. David Cheetham
11. George E. Bailey

CONSTABLES

1. Thomas Tunstall
2. William Barker
3. William Hallworth
4. Francis Moon
5. James Shadbolt
6. George Webster
7. William Leary
8. William Bicknell
9. James Storey
10. Edward Mitchell
11. James Orme
12. Joseph Bowers

13. James Barker
14. Peter Potts
15. Patrick Connor
16. Charles Harvey
17; William Moon
18. George Fountain
19. Frederick Leggett
20. James Henscol
21. William Hartley
22. Andrew McCrae
24. Thomas Calver
25. James Helliwell
26. Felix Meade
27. Thomas Greenwood
28. Thomas Lawson
29. Isaac Worthington
30. Henry Rowe
31. Thomas Kelly
32. William Senior
33. Henry Whittington
34. Thomas McCarthy
35. John Bowerman
36. John Roose
37. James Bold
38. Jeremiah Graham
39. John Dulton
40. Thomas Hulse
41. Samuel Matthews
42. Robert Skeet
43. William Ingram
44. John Potts
45. John Leach
46. William Sutherland
47. Isaac Wild
48. Ralph Mountford
49. Thomas Trelfa
50. John Thomas
51. Richard Jackson
52. Peter Pritchard
53. Joseph Larman

54. William Cartwright
55. Sidney Bouvier
56. George Vale
57. George Dunnicliffe
58. William Bray
59. Robert Hartley
60. John Coup
61. Elijah Coates
62. William Bate
63. John Fitzpatrick
64. Francis Storey
65. Edwin Hackney
66. William Mills
67. Thomas Johnson
68. John Soper
69. Thomas Hewitt
70. Peter Birtwistle
71. Thomas Clark
72. William Hargreaves
73. John Shaw
74. Albert Clarkson
75. Thomas Downes
76. James Heseltine
77. William Hockin
78. Joseph Hobson
79. James Barber
80. Frederick Boullen
82. John Scott
83. Patrick Carroll
84. Peter Gilinour
85. Hugh Kirby
86. John Kirk
87. John Littler
88. Joseph Wright
89. Charles Storey
90. Peter W. Foster
91. Henry S. Grew
92. Benjamin Crofsland
93. Thomas Blackburn
94. George Cantrell

95. John Twemlow
96. Samuel Nixon
97. Thomas Paton
98. Peter Foster
99. Thomas Henderson
100. Thomas McKay
101. Charles Beasley
102. William Jones
103. James Roberts
104. Benjamin Johnston
105. John Statham
106. Charles Newbold
107. Thomas Parker
108. George Ironmonger
109. John Reynolds
110. William Lace
111. Harry Grant
112. William Morley
113. James Brooks
114. James Gillespie
115. Robert Taylor
116. Thomas Hamson
117. Robert Martin
118. Robert B. Chidlow
119. James Neary
120. Heber Hayward
121. Samual Barker
122. George Norman
123. Henry Dodd
124. Thomas Bertenshaw
125. Thomas Lawson
126. William Dale
127. William Cawley

128. John Trevelyan
129. Richard Judd
130. Joseph Lambert
131. John Murphy
132. Edwin Roden
133. Joshua J. Graham
134. Arthur Spedding
135. Samuel Fox
136. James Reece
137. James Dutton
138. James Fibble
139. William Watson
140. Thomas McFarlane
141. Samuel Brailsford
142. James Wither
143. Henry Shepherd
144. John Groome
145. Charles Dickerson
146. Robert Fretwell
147. George Lewis
148. Peter Holbrook
149. Samuel Carrington
150. John H. Faulkner
151. Frederick Cookson
152. James F. Cornwall
153. David Telfer
154. Robert Welch
155. Thomas James
156. George Grafton
157. William Harper
159. Thomas Dowler
162. John Beddow

E   DIVISION

SUPERINTENDENT

Robert Coy

CHIEF INSPECTOR DETECTIVE DEPARTMENT

Robert Poole

CHIEF COURT INSPECTOR

Irving Watson

INSPECTORS

1. Andrew Thompson
2. Patrick Shandley
3. Thomas Gill
4. George Davenport
5. George Clayton
6. Aaron Rowbottom
7. Luke Holgate
8. Alexander Hornsby
9. Job Jones

SERGEANTS

1. Thomas Reddish
2. James Greenfield
3. Joseph Heaton
4. James Taylor
5. Henry Hirst
6. James Broome
7. Robert Bedford
8. Joseph Jackman
9. Charles Barlow
10. William Trueman

11. William McClelland
12. John Burniston
13. William E. Allanson
14. John Barlow
15. Fenton Haslam
16. Seth Bromley
17. Jerome Caminada

18. William Egan
19. Thomas Bramall
20. John Forr
21. William Slater
22. Frank Court
23. Edwin Hicks

CONSTABLES

1. Thomas Ashton
2. John Mather
3. Joseph Waterhouse
4. Thomas Nixon
5. Richard Cookson
6. James Connell
7. Thomas Lambert
8. John Frost
9. Richard Wood
10. John Beattie
11. Robert Fletcher
13. Henry Williams

14. Josiah Maund
15. Joseph Bloor
16. William Abbott
17. William Oldham
18. Samuel Robinson
19. James Smith
20. Richard Williamson
21. George H. Grubbe
22. George Hargreaves
23. Robert John Stansfield
24. George Howarth